Health and Safety R

The Essential NEBOSH Certificate Revision Guide

2014
Fully Revised

Richard Butler

Chartered Health and Safety Practitioner
with many years' experience of the
Health and Safety NEBOSH Qualification

Copyright

Copyright © 2014 and published by UK-HSE Ltd
www.safetytrainingunit.co.uk

Lulu Print Edition
ISBN: 978-1-291-80001-2

For anybody who is studying towards the NEBOSH qualification *'General Certificate in Occupational Safety and Health'*.

Also relevant to other NEBOSH certificate courses when there is a common syllabus e.g. International Certificate

Colour print copy, with photographs, available from
www.safetytrainingunit.co.uk

For more information about the National General Certificate and to obtain the full course guide visit
http://www.nebosh.org.uk

Introduction

I have written this book for anybody who is studying towards the NEBOSH National General Certificate in Occupational Safety and Health.

To be successful, you must have a good grasp of the requirements as laid out in the course guide produced by NEBOSH. This book will provide you with the essential learning.

Best of luck, and most important enjoy your studies.

Richard Butler
www.richardbutler.info

PS - any comments on the publication and how it can be improved are welcome. Please email info@uk-hse.co.uk

Contents

HEALTH AND SAFETY REVISION GUIDE 1
COPYRIGHT 2
INTRODUCTION 3
CONTENTS 4
CHAPTER 1 - FOUNDATIONS IN HEALTH AND SAFETY 15

   SECTION 1: IMPORTANT DEFINITIONS 16
      Learning Outcomes 16
      Definitions - must know! 16

   SECTION 2: REASONS FOR PROMOTING HEALTH AND SAFETY 17
      Learning Outcomes 17
      Drivers for health and Safety 17
      Direct costs of Accidents 19
      Indirect costs of Accidents 19
      Employers' liability insurance 20

   SECTION 3: LEGAL FRAMEWORK 21
      Learning Outcomes 21
      Sources of law 21
      Civil and Criminal Law - comparisons 22
      Court structure - where cases are heard 22
      Statute law 23
      Enforcing authorities 25
      Civil Law 28

   SECTION 4: SCOPE, DUTIES AND OFFENCES - HASAWA 31
      Learning Outcomes 31
      Employers' Duties to employees 31
      Employers' Duties to non-employees 32
      Employees' duties 32
      Managers' duties 32
      Duties of Designers, Manufacturers, Suppliers 33
      Duties of controllers of premises 33
      Offenses 33

   SECTION 5: SCOPE, DUTIES, OFFENCES - MANAGEMENT OF
   HEALTH AND SAFETY AT WORK REGULATIONS (MHSWR) 1999 34

Learning Outcomes *34*
Employers' Duties - MHSWR *34*
Employees' Duties - MHSWR *35*

SECTION 6: CLIENTS AND CONTRACTORS 35

Learning Outcomes *35*
Managing Contractors *36*
CDM Regulations *37*

CHAPTER 2 - HEALTH AND SAFETY MANAGEMENT SYSTEMS POLICY **45**

SECTION 1: KEY ELEMENTS OF A HSMS 46

Learning Outcomes *46*
Health and Safety Management System *46*
HSG 65 .... *47*

SECTION 2: PURPOSE OF SETTING POLICY 47

Learning Outcomes *47*
Purpose of Setting Policy *48*
Policy Review *48*

SECTION 3: STRUCTURE OF THE POLICY 49

Learning Outcomes *49*
Legal requirements *49*
Structure of the policy *50*

CHAPTER 3 - HEALTH AND SAFETY MANAGEMENT SYSTEMS ORGANISING **53**

SECTION 1: ROLES AND RESPONSIBILITIES 54

Learning Outcomes *54*
Employers *54*
Directors *55*
Safety advisor / competent person *55*
Managers / supervisors *56*
Controllers of premises *56*
Employees *56*
Self employed *57*

SECTION 2: CULTURE 57

Learning Outcomes *58*
Safety culture - definition *58*
Influences on culture *58*

Psychological factors 60
Effect of culture on performance 61
Improving Culture 61

SECTION 3: HUMAN FACTORS AND INFLUENCING BEHAVIOUR 62
Learning Outcomes 62
The three influencing factors 62
Human failure 64
Influencing behaviour 65

SECTION 4: HOW TO IMPROVE BEHAVIOUR 65
Learning Outcomes 65
Securing commitment 66
Competent persons 66
Effective communication 67
Training 70

SECTION 5: EMERGENCY PROCEDURES 72
Learning Outcomes 72
Importance of developing emergency procedures 72
Elements of emergency procedures 73

SECTION 6: PROVISION OF FIRST AID 74
Learning Outcomes 74
What is first aid? 74
First aid risk assessment 75
First aiders - numbers and type 75
Provision of first aid facilities 76

CHAPTER 4 - HEALTH AND SAFETY MANAGEMENT SYSTEMS PLANNING 77

SECTION 1: IMPORTANCE OF PLANNING.................................... 78
Learning Outcomes 78
Why planning is important 78
Setting objectives 78
Setting targets 79

SECTION 2: PRINCIPLES OF RISK ASSESSMENT 80
Learning Outcomes 80
What is risk assessment? 80
Hazard and risk 81
The risk assessment process 81
Competence of risk assessors 82

Special cases and vulnerable groups 83
SECTION 3: GENERAL PRINCIPLES OF RISK CONTROL 85
   Learning Outcomes 86
   General principles for risk reduction 86
   Hierarchy of control 86
   Suitable and sufficient risk control 87
   Evaluating adequacy of controls 87
SECTION 4: SOURCES OF INFORMATION 88
   Learning Outcomes 88
   Internal sources 88
   External sources 89
   Signs 90
   HSE Poster 90
SECTION 5: IMPLEMENTING A SAFE SYSTEM OF WORK 90
   Learning Outcomes 91
   Legal duties 91
   What is a safe system of work? 91
   Confined spaces 92
SECTION 6: PERMIT TO WORK (PTW) 93
   Learning Outcomes 93
   When is a PTW needed? 93
   Elements of a PTW 94
   Specific PTW 95

CHAPTER 5 - HEALTH AND SAFETY MANAGEMENT SYSTEMS MEASURING, REVIEW AND AUDITING 97
   SECTION 1: ACTIVE AND REACTIVE MONITORING 98
     Learning Outcomes 98
     Principles for monitoring 98
     Why monitor? 99
     Types of monitoring 100
   SECTION 2: HEALTH AND SAFETY AUDITING 102
     Learning Outcomes 102
     What is a health and safety audit? 102
     Scope of a health and safety audit 102
     Undertaking the audit 103
     Internal vs external auditing 104
   SECTION 3: INVESTIGATING ACCIDENTS 107

  Learning Outcomes *107*
  Why accidents and incidents occur *107*
  Investigation process... *108*
  Immediate and root causes... *111*
 SECTION 4: RECORDING AND REPORTING INCIDENTS 112
  Learning Outcomes *112*
  Why record accidents and incidents... *112*
  RIDDOR... *113*
 SECTION 5: REVIEW OF HEALTH AND SAFETY PERFORMANCE ... 114
  Learning Outcomes *114*
  Purpose of review... *114*
  Undertaking a review... *115*
  Records... *116*
  Reporting and feedback processes.. *116*

CHAPTER 6 - WORKPLACE HAZARDS AND RISK CONTROL 117

 SECTION 1: HEALTH, WELFARE AND WORK ENVIRONMENT
 REQUIREMENTS 118
  Learning Outcomes *118*
  Health and Welfare provisions.. *118*
  Temperature *122*
 SECTION 2: VIOLENCE AT WORK 123
  Learning Outcomes *123*
  What is violence?... *123*
  Control Measures *125*
  Risk Assessment - Violence.. *126*
 SECTION 3: SUBSTANCE MISUSE.. 126
  Learning Outcomes *126*
  Substance Misuse - Risk Factors.. *127*
  Control Measures *127*
 SECTION 4: SAFE MOVEMENT OF PEOPLE 128
  Learning Outcomes *128*
  Hazards in the workplace.. *128*
  Control measures - movement of people *131*
 SECTION 5: WORKING AT HEIGHT 134
  Learning Outcomes *134*
  Work activities involving working at height..................................... *134*

    Hazards and risks of working at height 135
    Generic control measures 135
    Ladders 136
    Fixed scaffolding 137
    Mobile tower - access platform 139
    Mobile elevated work platform 139
    Trestles 140
    Staging platforms 140
    Leading edge protection 141

  SECTION 6: EXCAVATIONS 142
    Learning Outcomes 142
    Hazards and risks of excavations 142
    Controls - excavations 143

CHAPTER 7 - TRANSPORT HAZARDS AND RISK CONTROLS 145

  SECTION 1: SAFE MOVEMENT OF VEHICLES 146
    Learning Outcomes 146
    Hazards from transport operations 146
    Common failings / control measures 147

  SECTION 2: DRIVING AT WORK 149
    Learning Outcomes 149
    Common Driving Hazards 149
    Control Measures - driving 150

CHAPTER 8 - MUSCULOSKELETAL HAZARDS AND RISK CONTROL ... 151

  SECTION 1: WORK RELATED UPPER LIMB DISORDERS 152
    Learning Outcomes 152
    Risk factors 152
    Types of injury 153
    Display Screen Equipment (DSE) 154
    DSE Risk assessment 156

  SECTION 2: MANUAL HANDLING 157
    Learning Outcomes 157
    Common types of injury 158
    Manual handling assessment 159
    Effective lifting technique 160

  SECTION 3: MECHANICALLY OPERATED LIFTING AND MOVING EQUIPMENT 161

Learning Outcomes *161*
Hazards and risks of common types of loading equipment *161*

SECTION 4: LIFTING AND MOVING EQUIPMENT 162
Learning Outcomes *162*
General considerations *163*
Statutory inspection and testing *164*
Fork Lift Trucks (FLTs) *165*
Lifts and hoists *167*
Conveyors *167*
Steel rollers *168*
Cranes *168*

CHAPTER 9 - WORK EQUIPMENT HAZARDS AND RISK CONTROL.... 171

SECTION 1: GENERAL REQUIREMENTS OF WORK EQUIPMENT ... 172
Learning Outcomes *172*
Scope of work equipment *172*
Suitability of work equipment *172*
Machine control systems *173*
Provision of information, instruction and supervision *174*
Machine maintenance *174*
Examination and Testing *175*
Pressure Systems *175*

SECTION 2: HAND HELD TOOLS 176
Learning Outcomes *176*
Hazards and risks of hand-held tools *176*

SECTION 3: MACHINERY HAZARDS 177
Learning Outcomes *177*
Mechanical and non-mechanical hazards *177*
Chain saw *179*
Photocopier *179*
Document Shredder *179*
Portable electric drill *180*
Cement Mixer *180*
Portable electric sander *181*
Bench top grinder *181*
Bench Mounted Drill *181*
Strimmer *182*
Compactor/bailer *182*

SECTION 4: CONTROL MEASURES FOR REDUCING RISKS 182

Learning Outcomes *182*
Basic principles of machine guarding *183*
Types of Guard *183*
Other machine protection devices *185*

CHAPTER 10 - ELECTRICAL SAFETY **187**

S<small>ECTION</small> 1: P<small>RINCIPLES OF ELECTRICITY</small> 188
Learning Outcomes *188*
Principles of electricity *188*
Effects of electricity *189*
Treatment of electric shock *189*
The main causes of electrical fires in the workplace *190*

S<small>ECTION</small> 2: C<small>ONTROL MEASURES</small> 190
Learning Outcomes *191*
General Controls - electricity *191*
Electrical safety devices *192*
Safe use of portable electrical equipment *193*
Overhead power cables *193*
Buried services *194*

CHAPTER 11 - FIRE SAFETY **195**

S<small>ECTION</small> 1: F<small>IRE - BASIC PRINCIPLES, HAZARDS AND RISKS</small> 196
Learning outcomes *196*
Responsible person *196*
Regulatory Reform (Fire Safety) Order 2005 .... *196*
The Fire Triangle *197*
Classification of fires *198*
Principles of heat transfer *198*
Common causes of fires *198*

S<small>ECTION</small> 2: F<small>IRE RISK ASSESSMENT</small> 199
Learning Outcomes *199*
Fire risk assessment - process *199*

S<small>ECTION</small> 3: F<small>IRE ALARM AND FIRE-FIGHTING EQUIPMENT</small> 201
Learning Outcomes *201*
Fire detection and warning *201*
Fire-fighting equipment *202*

S<small>ECTION</small> 4: E<small>VACUATION OF THE WORKPLACE</small> 204
Learning Outcomes *204*

Emergency procedures *204*
Roles of fire wardens *205*
Provision of information *205*
Building requirements *206*

SECTION 5: HIGHLY FLAMMABLE LIQUIDS 207
Learning Outcomes *207*
Safe storage *207*
Safe use *208*

CHAPTER 12 - CHEMICAL AND BIOLOGICAL HEALTH HAZARDS AND CONTROL 209

SECTION 1: FORMS AND CLASSIFICATION OF HAZARDOUS SUBSTANCES 210
Learning Outcomes *210*
Chemical forms *210*
Biological forms *210*
Sources of information *212*

SECTION 2: ASSESSMENT OF HEALTH RISKS 214
Learning Outcomes *214*
Routes of entry into the body *215*
Assessments - factors to consider *217*

SECTION 3: WORKPLACE EXPOSURE LIMITS (WELs) 217
Learning Outcomes *217*
Purpose of Work Exposure Limits (WELs) *218*
Threshold limit values *218*

SECTION 4: CONTROL MEASURES 218
Learning Outcomes *218*
Principles of good practice *219*
LEV systems *220*

SECTION 5: SPECIFIC AGENTS 220
Learning Outcomes *221*
Asbestos *221*
Blood born viruses *223*
Carbon monoxide (CO) *223*
Cement *224*
Legionella *224*
Leptospirosis *225*
Silica *225*

  Hard and soft wood dusts *226*
 Section 6: Safe handling and storage of waste 226
  Learning Outcomes *226*
  Principles of storage *226*

CHAPTER 13 - PHYSICAL AND PSYCHOLOGICAL HEALTH HAZARDS AND RISK CONTROL **229**

 Section 1: Noise 230
  Learning Outcomes *230*
  Noise - basic principles *230*
  Typical noise levels *232*
  Control of noise *232*
 Section 2: Vibration 234
  Learning Outcomes *234*
  Whole body vibration *234*
  Control of vibration *236*
 Section 3: Radiation 237
  Learning Outcomes *237*
  Types and sources of radiation *237*
  Radon *239*
 Section 4: Stress 240
  Learning Outcomes *240*
  Causes and effects of stress *240*
  Risk assessment and control of stress *241*

ABOUT THE AUTHOR **245**

Chapter 1 - Foundations in Health and Safety

Section 1: Important definitions

In this section:

1. Definitions - must know!

Learning Outcomes

Outline the scope and nature of occupational health and safety

Definitions - must know!

Health - state of complete physical, mental and social well-being and not merely the absence of disease or infirmity.

Safety - state of being safe i.e. free from the unacceptable risk of injury, danger or loss.

Welfare - the provision of facilities for the wellbeing of employees, such as; washing, toilet, rest and changing facilities and somewhere clean to eat and drink during breaks.

Occupational health - the promotion and maintenance of the highest degree of physical, mental and social wellbeing of workers in all occupations.

Hazard - something with the potential to cause harm e.g. uneven floor surface, working at a height.

Risk - the chance or likelihood that a hazard will cause harm along with the severity of the consequence.

Likelihood / severity - the chance that harm will occur and the severity of the harm.

Accident - an unplanned or an unwanted event that resulted in a loss or harm e.g. personal injury, equipment damage.

Incident / near miss - an unplanned or an unwanted event that had the potential to result in loss or harm.

Work related ill health - the hazards that an individual has been exposed to during his/her working life which have had a detrimental effect to their health and quality of life.

Section 2: Reasons for promoting health and safety

In this section:

1. Drivers for health and Safety
2. Direct costs of Accidents
3. Indirect costs of Accidents
4. Employers liability insurance

Learning Outcomes

Explain the moral, social and economic reasons for promoting good standards of health and safety in the workplace

Drivers for health and Safety

There are three basic categories:

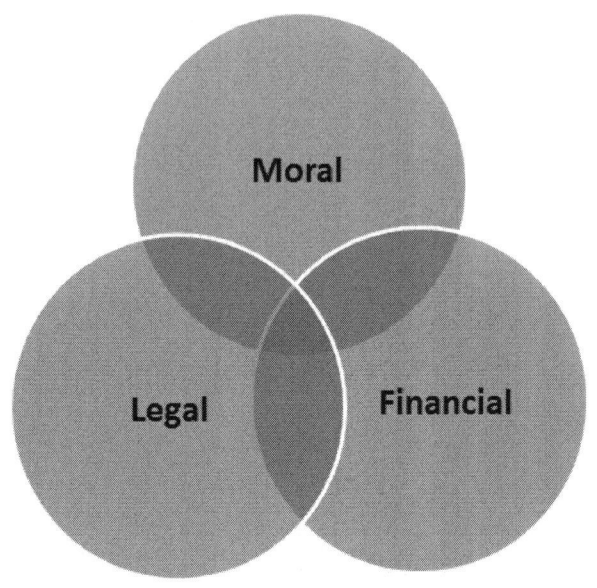

Moral / social / ethical reasons

- prevention of harm to people e.g. colleagues, friends etc.
- incident / accident rates reduced / prevented
- industrial disease and ill health rates reduced / prevented
- improved safety culture and workers' moral increased
- requirement to provide safe place of work, safe plant and equipment, safe systems, provisions of welfare facilities
- publicity and image improved

Legal - see later section for more details

- non-compliance to laws - prosecutions and enforcement actions if non-compliant
- civil actions - compensation claims if harm caused to people, property or environment

Financial /cost - see later section for more details

- direct costs
- indirect costs

Direct costs of Accidents

Insured - direct costs

- claims on employers and public liability insurance
- damage to buildings, equipment or vehicles
- any attributable production and/or general business loss

Uninsured - direct costs

- fines resulting from prosecution by the enforcement authority
- sick pay
- some damage to product, equipment, vehicles or process not directly attributable to the accident (e.g. caused by replacement staff)
- increases in insurance premiums resulting from the accident
- any compensation not covered by the insurance policy due to an excess agreed between the employer and the insurance company
- legal representation following any compensation claim

Indirect costs of Accidents

Insured - indirect costs

- a cumulative business loss
- product or process liability claims
- recruitment of replacement staff

Uninsured - indirect costs

- loss of goodwill and that poor corporate image
- accident investigation time and any subsequent remedial action required
- production delays
- extra overtime payments
- lost time for other employees, such as first aide, who attended to the needs of the injured person
- the recruitment and training of replacement staff
- additional and administration time incurred
- first aid provision and training
- no employee morale possibly leading to reduced productivity

Costs Summary

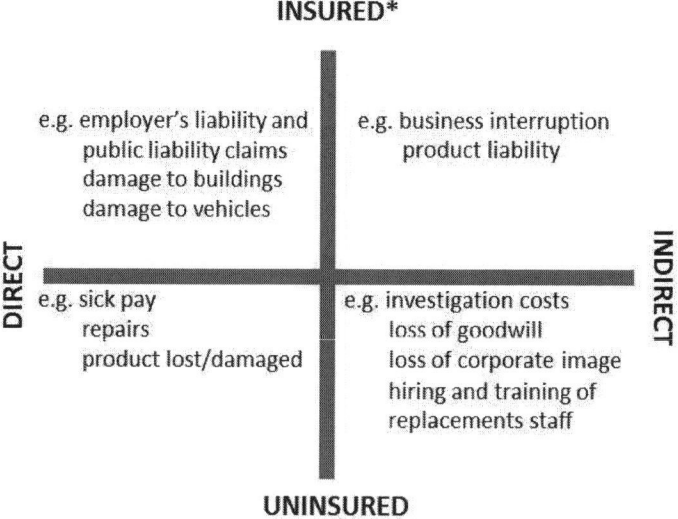

Source - HSE

Employers' liability insurance

- legal requirement to cover all employers
- minimum of £5 million

- covers employers' liability (insured costs) of accidents and incidents
- must be displayed, or made readily available, within the workplace

Section 3: Legal framework

In this section:

1. Sources of law
2. Civil and criminal law - comparisons
3. Court structure - civil and criminal
4. Statute law
5. Enforcing authorities
6. Civil law

Learning Outcomes

Explain the legal framework for the regulation of health and safety including sources and types of law

Sources of law

Common Law	Statute Law
Based on the judgements (decisions) by judges in court - often called judicial precedent	The law of the land, written by Parliament - e.g. The Health and Safety at Work Act and Regulations
Courts are bound by the judgements	Specific duties are contained with Regulations
Lower courts follow the judgements of a higher court	Takes precedent over Common Law
Definitions or interpretations of terminology are based on judicial precedent e.g. *'negligence'*, *'So Far As Is Reasonably Practicable'*	A breach of statutory duty can be used in the civil courts as a demonstration of negligence

Civil and Criminal Law - comparisons

Civil Law	Criminal Law
Tort - i.e. negligence	Crime; a breach of law e.g. The Health and Safety at Work Act or a Regulation
Civil wrong	Criminal offense to breach the law of the land and prosecuted by the state
Wrong to an individual	Offense against society
Cases 'heard' in the civil court	Cases 'heard' in the criminal courts; firstly the magistrates court
Loss is necessary for action to be taken	Loss is not necessary for action to be taken
Wronged person seeks compensation for loss	If found guilty the outcome is punishment e.g. fine
Cases decided on the 'Balance of Probability'	Cases decided 'Beyond Reasonable Doubt'
Employer can insure against the loss (Employers' Liability Insurance)	Cannot insure against outcome

Court structure - where cases are heard

England, Wales and Northern Ireland

- **Civil Cases** – heard in Civil Courts; initially County Court
- **Criminal Cases** – heard in Criminal Courts; initially Magistrates Court and then possibly sent to the Crown Court

Scotland

- **Criminal Cases** – the most serious cases involving trial on indictment before a judge or sheriff sitting with a jury in the Sheriff Court. Less serious offences (summary) involving a trial before a sheriff, stipendiary magistrate or Justice of the Peace sitting alone

- **Civil Cases** – heard in the Court of Session

Industrial tribunals

- established to take decisions in particular areas of law
- health and safety - to hear appeals against Improvement and Prohibition Notices
- refusal to work: employees protected by Employment Rights Act 1996 where there is serious, imminent and unavoidable danger

Statute law

Statute Law is the 'law of the land' and consists of **Acts**, **Regulations** and **Orders**.

Approved Codes of Practice (ACoPs)

- produced by the Health and Safety Executive to give practical interpretation of specific Regulations - note all Regulations do not have ACoPs
- can be used as evidence in court, therefore 'quasi legal' status
- provides example of best practice

Guidance

- interpretation of how a task or activity could be carried out
- produced by the HSE and professional organisations

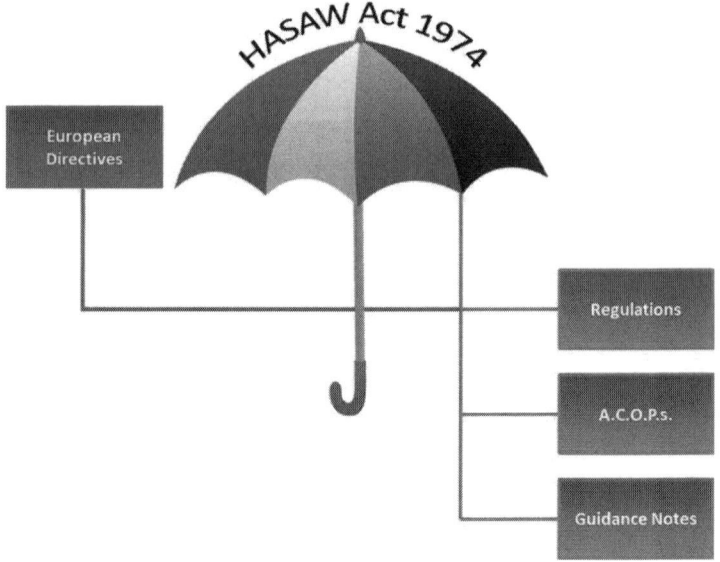

Absolute and qualified duties

Absolute duty - the employer MUST comply with the law, irrespective of associated costs with wording within the Regulations as - 'must', 'will' or 'shall'; which implies an Absolute duty to Comply. For example:

- RIDDOR requires the reporting of specific injuries, dangerous occurrences and diseases
- HASAWA requires an employer, who employs more than 5 people, to produce a written safety policy

So Far as is Practicable - must comply if technology is available or it is technically possible

So Far as is Reasonably Practicable – balance of Risk against Cost e.g. Section 2 of HASAWA requires an employer to set up safe systems 'so far as is reasonably practicable'

- **Risk** – combination of likelihood and severity

- **Cost** – in terms of 'time, money and trouble'

Enforcing authorities

The **Health and Safety Executive** (HSE) is the enforcing authority for Health and Safety.

- **Local Authority** (LA) enforce Health and Safety legislation in offices and shops, and some Environmental legislation

- **Office of Rail Regulator** (ORR), **Nuclear Inspectorate, Inspection of Mines and Offshore Regulator** are all branches of the HSE enforcing Health and Safety legislation in the respective areas

- **The Fire Service** enforce Fire Safety legislation

- **The Environment Agency** (EA) enforce Environmental Legislation

Role of HSE and HSC

The **Health and Safety Commission** (HSC), directly reportable to the Minister, sets policy and oversees the HSE.

The **Health and Safety Executive** (HSE) is the enforcing authority for Health and Safety legislation, but also promotes and makes available good practice via their website and publications. The HSE and HSC jointly:

- advise on the development of Regulations
- enforce health and safety legislation
- provide information to organisations and produce ACoPs, guidance notes, leaflets and other publications
- compile accident and ill-health statistics

- launch national health and safety campaigns on specific topics
- carry out accident and other investigations and collate statistics
- offer advice to employers / others on statutory duties
- take enforcement action (HSE)
- publicise organisations that receive enforcement notices

Fire service

- undertake random fire inspections (often to examine fire risk assessments)
- can issue alteration, improvement and prohibition notices
- need to be informed during the planning stage of building alterations if fire safety of the building may be affected

Local Authority (LA)

- enforce health and safety legislation in offices and shops
- enforce environmental legislation (some) e.g. noise nuisance
- LAs also enforce other primary legislation relating to pesticides (Food and Environment Protection Act 1985) on a similar basis, as well as storage of explosives and petroleum licensing

Environmental Agency (EA)

- responsible for authorising and regulating emissions from industry
- ensuring effective controls of the most polluting industries monitoring radioactive releases from nuclear sites
- ensuring that discharges to controlled waters are at acceptable levels

- setting standards and issuing permits for the collection, transporting, processing and disposal of waste (including radioactive waste)

Powers of Inspectors

The Powers of Inspectors can be summarised as follows:

- entry at any reasonable time (or at any time if dangerous situation arises)
- take a police constable
- take any other person and any equipment
- order that areas are left undisturbed
- take measurements, photographs and samples
- carry out tests on articles or substances
- confiscate articles or substances
- inspect and take copies of relevant documents
- seize any article or substance which presents an immediate danger of serious personal injury
- interview and take written statements
- can issue improvement and prohibition notices

Inspectors Actions - notices, advice and prosecution

Notices

Inspectors can issue two types of notices:

Improvement notice

- served if an employer has failed to comply with statute law
- requires the breach to be remedied within a set period of time

- allows for an appeal, to be made within 21 days. If under appeal, the notice is suspended until the appeal is resolved

Prohibition notice

- instruction to stop doing something (activity or use of equipment)
- served where a serious risk of personal injury has occurred or is likely to occur
- identifies breaches of the law and prevents the activity from taking place
- appeal is allowed within 21 days but the enforcement will stay in place while the appeal is heard

Advice

Inspectors can give verbal or written advice

Prosecution

Inspectors can prosecute for breach of legislation

Civil Law

In Civil Law, the employer has a Duty of Care to employees, visitors and contractors. Case Law has 'defined' Duty of Care as:

- a safe place of work
- safe plant and equipment
- a safe system of work
- safe and competent fellow employees

Civil wrong

If the above are not provided; there is a Civil Wrong (or Tort) and compensation can be awarded if the wrong is proved

Any action must commence within three years of harm (injury) or when party (harmed / injured person) becomes aware that injury has been caused by employer

Foreseeable

Three 'tests' are required to demonstrate if something is reasonably foreseeable, they are:

- **common knowledge** - i.e. what is the collective common knowledge of the general public. This is often referred to as the common knowledge of the person who rides the 'Clapham Omnibus'

- **expert knowledge** i.e. what should an expert be expected to know

- **specialist knowledge** i.e. what should a specialist in the subject be expected to know

Negligence

Negligence is:

- lack of reasonable care or conduct resulting in harm and must be reasonably foreseeable that the acts or omissions could result in harm

Contributory negligence occurs when a person 'contributes' to their own injury

Defense of negligence

Proving Negligence	
Defense	**Partial Defense**
The Duty of Care was not owned	Contributory negligence - employee contributed to the negligent act
There was not a breach of Duty of Care	Volenti No Fit Injury - the risk was willingly accepted by the employee
The breach of Duty of Care did not cause the harm	Any breach of the Duty of Care resulted in a specific injury, disease, damage and/or loss
Employee *'on a frolic of his own'*	

Breach of Statutory Duty

A tort / negligence occurs if:

- there is a statuary duty owed e.g. requirement of a Regulation (but not all)
- there is a breach of the statutory duty
- the harm was a result of the breach

Breach usually linked with a claim of negligence - called double barrelled approach

Vicarious liability

The employer is responsible for the acts and omissions of the employee whilst they are 'at work' - i.e. employer is responsible for torts of servants (employees) in the course of employment whether authorised or not.

Section 4: Scope, duties and offences - HASAWA

In this Section:

1. Employers' duties
2. Employees' duties
3. Managers' duties
4. Manufacturers', Designers and Importers' duties
5. Occupiers' duties
6. Offences

Learning Outcomes

Explain the scope, duties and offenses of employers, managers, employees and others under the Health and Safety at Work etc. Act 1974 (HASAWA)

Employers' Duties to employees

Ensure, So Far as is Reasonably Practicable:

- health, safety and welfare at work of all employees
- safe plant and safe systems of work
- safe systems for the use, handling, storage and transport of articles and substances
- information, instruction, training and supervision
- safe place of work with safe access and egress
- healthy working environment and adequate welfare provision

Absolute Duties under the Act:

- employer cannot charge an employee for anything done or provided to comply with health and safety legislation e.g. provide Personal Protective Equipment
- if more than 5 employees, prepare and communicate a written Safety Policy
- communicate with Trades' Unions and Representatives and form a Safety Committee

Employers' Duties to non-employees

Ensure So Far as is Reasonably Practicable

- persons not in his (or her) employment, who may be affected by their acts of omissions, are not exposed to risks to their health and safety

Employees' duties

Ensure So Far as is Reasonably Practicable

- take care for the health and safety of themselves and of other persons who may be affected by their work
- co-operate with his employer so far as is necessary to enable the employer to comply with his own duties
- to not intentionally or recklessly interfere with or misuse anything provided in the interests of health, safety or welfare

Managers' duties

Ensure So Far as is Reasonably Practicable

- persons working under their control are working safely

Note - a manager is anybody who controls work activities, and can be a Director or Company Secretary.

Duties of Designers, Manufacturers, Suppliers

Ensure So Far as is Reasonably Practicable

- any article or substance is safe and without risks to health when properly used
- any necessary research / testing / examination is properly undertaken
- adequate information is provided to ensure article or substance is safe to use

Duties of controllers of premises

Ensure So Far as is Reasonably Practicable

- premises are safe and without risk

Offenses

If a breach of HASAWA or a Regulation is proved a court can impose the following:

Breach	Magistrates Court	Crown Court
HASAWA Section 2-8	Term not exceeding 12 months and/or Fine not exceeding £20,000	Term not exceeding 2 years and/or unlimited fine
Regulations	Term not exceeding 12 months and/or fine not exceeding £20,000	Term not exceeding 2 years and/or unlimited fine

Section 5: Scope, duties, offences - Management of Health and Safety at Work Regulations (MHSWR) 1999

In this Section:

1. Employers' duties
2. Employees' duties

Learning Outcomes

Explain the scope, duties and offences of employers, managers, employees and others under the Management of Health and Safety at Work Regulations

Employers' Duties - MHSWR

The Management Regulations require: to

- undertake a suitable and sufficient risk assessment
- implement preventive and protective measures (based on principles specified in Schedule 1)
- put in place effective health and safety management arrangements
- employ a competent health and safety person
- develop suitable emergency arrangements
- provide health and safety information to employees and others, such as
- other employers, the self-employed and their employees who are sharing the same workplace
- those on work experience e.g. from school, college, training organisation
- co-operate in health and safety matters with other employers who share the same workplace

- provide employees with adequate and relevant health and safety training
- provide temporary workers and their contract agency with appropriate health and safety information
- protect new and expectant mothers and young persons from particular risks
- under certain circumstances provide health surveillance for employees
- provide information to employers e.g.
- details of risk assessments and the preventative and protective measures that are in place

Employees' Duties - MHSWR

- use items provided by the employer (including both machinery and safety equipment) in accordance with the training and instructions that the employer provides
- to notify employers of any serious hazards that they may encounter
- where appointed safety representatives exist, employees can report such matters to them, to discharge their duty under this regulation.

Section 6: Clients and contractors

In this Section:

1. Managing contractors
2. The Construction (Design and Management) Regulations (CDM) 2007

Learning Outcomes

Outline the legal and organisational health and safety roles and responsibilities of clients and their contractors

Managing Contractors

The managing contractors is a **5-step** process

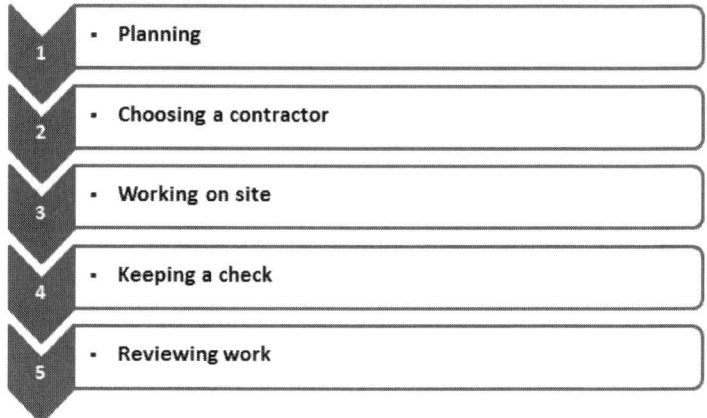

1. Planning

- define the job; risk management; specifying conditions

2. Choosing a Contractor

- consider; availability, cost, technical competence, reliability, health, safety and environment competence, references, previous work

3. Working on Site

- manage contractors movements; visitor controls, Permit to Work, risk assessments, method statements
- technical and management controls (Work equipment, PPE, Safe Systems of Work etc.
- information, instruction and training - competence of specific employees/contractors
- co-operation; co-ordination; consultation; supervision

4. **Keeping a Check**

- frequency proportionate to risk; contractor's daily checks; client periodic checks; action to address problems

5. **Reviewing the Work**

- effectiveness of planning; contractor performance; how smoothly the job went

CDM Regulations

The Construction (Design and Management) Regulations (CDM) 2007 applies to ALL constructions sites.

Notifiable

The HSE must be notified if construction:

- lasts more than 30 working days; OR
- involves more than 500 person days, for example 50 people working for over 10 days

Client Duties - as detailed within the CDM Regulations

ALL Projects	ADDITIONAL duties for notifiable
Check competence and resources of all appointees	Appoint CDM Co-ordinator
Ensure there are suitable management arrangements for the project including welfare facilities	Appoint principal contractor
Allow sufficient time and resources for all stages	Make sure that the construction phase does not start until: 1. welfare facilitates are provided 2. construction phase plan is in place
Provide pre-construction information to designers and contractors	Provide information relating to the health and safety file to the CDM Coordinator
Check competence and resources of all appointees	Retain and provide access to the health and safety file

Designer duties - as detailed within the CDM Regulations

ALL Projects	ADDITIONAL duties for notifiable
Check client is aware of their duties	Check CDM Co-ordinator has been appointed
Eliminate hazards and reduce risks during design	Provide any information needed for the health and safety file
Provide information about remaining risks	

CDM Coordinator (CDMC) duties - as detailed within the CDM Regulations

Only have duties for NOTIFIABLE (NOT appointed for non-notifiable)
Advise and assist the client with their duties
Notify HSE
Co-ordinate health and safety of design work and co-operate with others involved with the project
Facilitate good communication between client, designers and contractors
Liaise with principal contractor regarding ongoing design
Identify, collect and pass on pre-construction information
Prepare/update health and safety file

Principal Contractor (PC) duties - as detailed within the CDM Regulations

Only have duties for NOTIFIABLE (NOT appointed for non-notifiable)
Plan, manage and monitor construction phase in liaison with contractor
Prepare, develop and implement a written plan and site rules. (Initial plan completed before the construction phase begins)
Give contractors relevant parts of the plan
Make sure suitable welfare facilities are provided from the start and maintained throughout the construction phase
Check competence of all appointees
Consult with the workers
Liaise with CDM Co-ordinator regarding ongoing design
Secure the site
Ensure all workers have site inductions and any further information and training needed for the work

Contractor duties - as detailed within the CDM Regulations

ALL Projects	ADDITIONAL duties for notifiable
Check client is aware of their duties	Check a CDM co-ordinator and a principal contractor have been appointed and HSE notified before starting work
Plan, manage and monitor own work and that of workers	Co-operate with principal contractor in planning and managing work, including reasonable directions and site rules
Check competence of all their appointees and workers	Provide details to the principal contractor of any contractor whom he engages in connection with carrying out the work
Train own employees	Inform principal contractor of problems with the plan
Provide information to their workers	Provide any information needed for the health and safety file
Comply with the specific requirements in Part 4 of the Regulations	Inform principal contractor of reportable accidents, diseases and dangerous occurrences
Ensure there are adequate welfare facilities for their workers	

Notification to HSE

If a construction project is notifiable the information that has to be sent to HSE is:

Information includes

- date of forwarding
- exact address of the construction site
- name of the local authority where the site is located
- brief description of the project and the construction work which it includes
- contact details of the client, CDM Co-ordinator, designer(s) and principal contractor
- date planned for the start of the construction phase
- time allowed by the client to the principal contractor for construction and planning

- estimated maximum number of people at work on the construction site
- declaration signed by or on behalf of the client that they (client) are aware of their duties

Note - the information is usually supplied by completing the HSE's F10 form or electronically via the HSE's website

Pre-construction information

Provides information for those bidding for or planning work and for the development of the construction phase plan.

Description of project

- project description and programme
- details of Client, Designers, CDM Co-ordinator and other Consultants and whether or not the structure will be used as a workplace
- the extent and location of existing records and plans

Client's considerations and management requirements

- arrangements for; planning, communication, liaison, security and welfare
- specific H&S requirements e.g. site hoarding, transport or vehicle movement restrictions, fire precautions, emergency procedures and means of escape, 'no-go' areas, any areas the client has designated as confined spaces and smoking and parking restrictions.

Environmental restrictions and existing on-site risks

- safety hazards e.g. existing storage of hazardous materials, ground conditions, reference to underground structures

or water courses, information contained in earlier design stages
- health hazards e.g. asbestos, contaminated land, health risks from client's activities

Significant design and construction hazards

- significant design assumptions and suggested work methods, sequences or other control measures
- information on significant risks identified during design and materials requiring particular precautions
- arrangements for co-ordination of ongoing design work and handling design changes

Health and safety file

- description of its format

Construction Phase Plan (CPP)

The CPP is developed by the Principal Contractor from the Pre-construction Information. Typical contents include:

Description of project

- programme details, key dates, details of client, CDM Co-ordinator, designers, principal contractor and other consultants;
- extent and location of existing records and plans

Management of work

- management structure and responsibilities
- health and safety goals for the project
- management arrangements e.g. exchange of health and safety information (e.g. between CDMC, Designers and

other Contractors), site security, site induction, competence of all on site, welfare facilities, first aid arrangements, reporting and investigation of accidents and incidents, emergency procedures etc.
- arrangements for controlling significant risks e.g. delivery and removal of materials (waste), risks to the public, access to or egress from the site, dealing with services - water, electricity and gas, including overhead powerlines, stability of structures whilst carrying out construction work, preventing falls, control of lifting operations, work on excavations and work where there are poor ground conditions, traffic, environmental considerations etc.
- arrangements for controlling health risks e.g. removal of asbestos, manual handling, hazardous substances, control of noise and vibration, ionising radiation etc.

Health and Safety File

For notifiable projects the CDM Co-ordinator must prepare a suitable Health and Safety File and present to the client at the end of the project. The file is

- a source of information that will help to reduce the risks and costs involved in future construction work, including cleaning, maintenance, alterations, refurbishment and demolition

Chapter 2 - Health and Safety Management Systems Policy

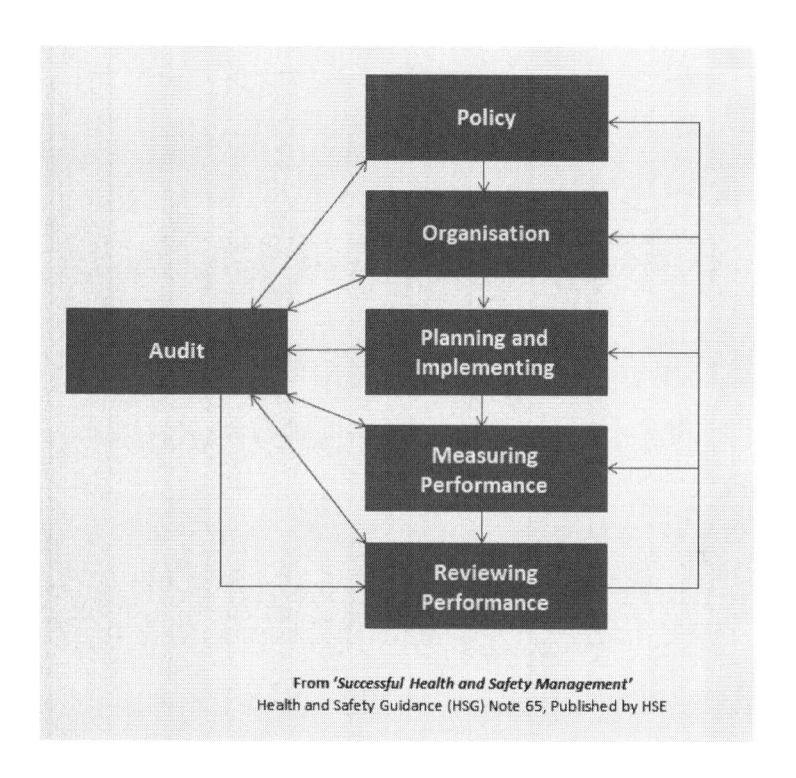

```
                    ┌──────────────┐
                    │    Policy    │◄─────┐
                    └──────┬───────┘      │
                           ▼              │
                    ┌──────────────┐      │
                    │ Organisation │◄─────┤
                    └──────┬───────┘      │
                           ▼              │
  ┌─────────┐       ┌──────────────┐      │
  │  Audit  │◄─────►│ Planning and │◄─────┤
  │         │       │ Implementing │      │
  └─────────┘       └──────┬───────┘      │
                           ▼              │
                    ┌──────────────┐      │
                    │  Measuring   │◄─────┤
                    │ Performance  │      │
                    └──────┬───────┘      │
                           ▼              │
                    ┌──────────────┐      │
                    │  Reviewing   │──────┘
                    │ Performance  │
                    └──────────────┘
```

From *'Successful Health and Safety Management'*
Health and Safety Guidance (HSG) Note 65, Published by HSE

Section 1: Key elements of a HSMS

In this Section:

1. Health and Safety Management System - HSMS
2. Successful Health and Safety Management (HSG 65)

Learning Outcomes

Outline the key elements of a health and safety management system

Health and Safety Management System

The general framework for Health and Safety Management as recommended by the HSE is:

Policy

- the policy should state the intentions of the organization in terms of clear aims, objectives, targets and senior management involvement

Organising

- a well-defined health and safety organization should identify health and safety responsibilities at all levels of the organization.

Planning and implementing

- a clear health and safety plan based on risk assessment, sets and implements performance standards, targets and procedures

Measuring performance

- This includes both active (sometimes called proactive) and reactive

Reviewing performance

- the results of monitoring and independent audits should indicate whether the objectives and targets set in the health and safety policy need to be changed

Auditing

- to identify weaknesses in the health and safety management system

HSG 65

HSG 65 (Health and Safety Guidance note 65) is the reference number of the publication 'Successful Health and Safety Management' produced by the HSE. It is guidance which provides a step-by-step method of managing for health and safety

Section 2: Purpose of setting policy

In this section:

1. Purpose of setting policy
2. Policy review

Learning Outcomes

Explain the purpose and importance of setting policy for health and safety

Purpose of Setting Policy

The purpose of setting a policy can be summarised as follows:

- it is a legal requirement
- supports the overall development of personnel
- defines roles and responsibilities
- improves communication and consultation throughout the organization
- minimizes financial losses due to accidents and ill-health and other incidents
- directly involves senior managers in all parts of the organisation
- improves the public image of the organization
- defines the health and safety arrangements for:
- planning and organising for health and safety and performance
- the effective controlling of hazards and risks
- ensuring consultation, competence, communication, cooperation and monitoring
- assessing the effectiveness of the arrangements to implement the health and safety policy

Policy Review

A Health and Safety Policy should be reviewed when:

- there are significant organisational changes occur e.g. moving premises, implementation of a revised organisational structure
- there are significant changes in personnel and/or legislation
- health and safety performance has fallen below the occupational group's benchmarks

- the monitoring of risk assessments and/or accident/incident investigations indicate that the health and safety policy may not be effective
- there is the introduction of significant new plant or equipment
- there are significant changes in processes
- the policy is no longer totally effective
- the findings of audits and/or appropriate monitoring indicates it is no longer effective or fit for purpose
- enforcement action has been taken by the Enforcing Authority
- consultation with managers, unions or worker representatives indicates the policy is not effective
- a sufficient period of time has elapsed since the previous review

Section 3: Structure of the Policy

In this section:

1. Legal requirements
2. The structure of a policy

Learning Outcomes

Describe the key features and appropriate content of an effective health and safety policy

Legal requirements

The Health and Safety at Work Act 1974 requires every employer whom employs five persons or more, to prepare and provide a written Health and Safety Policy and to effectively communicate that policy to his/her employees.

Structure of the policy

An organisation's Health and Safety Policy will consist of 3 fundamental parts:

Statement

This section details what the organisation's intentions are regarding Health and Safety. The statement is a fundamental and crucial part of any business planning by setting out the minimum aims, objectives and standards which demonstrates the organisation's commitment towards.

Organisation

The organisation section details how and who in the organisation is/are responsible and for what.

Arrangements

This section will detail the scope of the organisation's systems and procedures. Examples of arrangements are:

- Accident/Incident Investigation and Reporting
- Audits, Inspections and Monitoring
- First Aid At Work

Key features of an effective policy statement

The key features of an effective policy statement are, it:

- includes aims and objectives for health, safety and welfare
- includes duties of employer and employees to each other and the wider public and others
- includes performance targets for the immediate and long-term future

- benchmarks performance
- includes the name and post of the person responsible for the management of health and safety in the organisation
- is signed and dated by the most senior person in the organisation
- includes a date by which the statement will be reviewed
- is posted on prominent notice boards throughout the workplace

Chapter 3 - Health and Safety Management Systems Organising

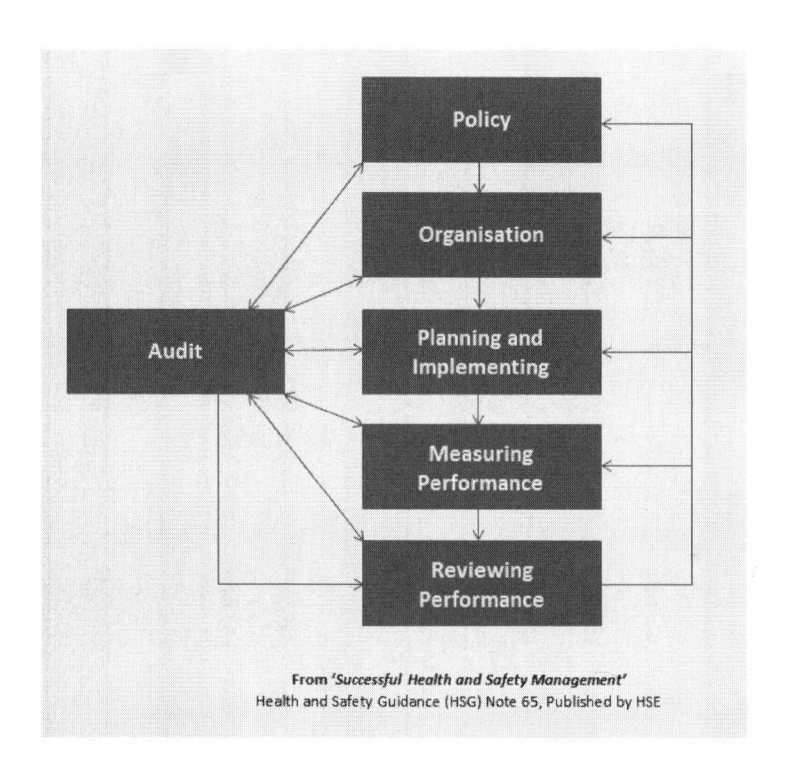

```
                    ┌──────────────┐
                    │    Policy    │◄─────┐
                    └──────┬───────┘      │
                           ▼              │
                    ┌──────────────┐      │
                    │ Organisation │◄─────┤
                    └──────┬───────┘      │
                           ▼              │
┌──────────┐        ┌──────────────┐      │
│          │───────►│ Planning and │◄─────┤
│  Audit   │◄───────│ Implementing │      │
│          │        └──────┬───────┘      │
│          │               ▼              │
│          │        ┌──────────────┐      │
│          │───────►│  Measuring   │◄─────┤
│          │◄───────│ Performance  │      │
│          │        └──────┬───────┘      │
│          │               ▼              │
│          │        ┌──────────────┐      │
│          │───────►│  Reviewing   │      │
│          │◄───────│ Performance  │──────┘
└──────────┘        └──────────────┘
```

From *'Successful Health and Safety Management'*
Health and Safety Guidance (HSG) Note 65, Published by HSE

Section 1: Roles and responsibilities

In this section:

1. Employers
2. Directors
3. Safety advisor / competent person
4. Managers / supervisors
5. Controllers of premises
6. Employees
7. Self employed

Learning Outcomes

Outline the health and safety roles and responsibilities of employers, managers, supervisors, workers and other relevant parties

The duties of employers, employee etc. are detailed within the legislation, specifically HASAWA and Regulations. This section details the roles and responsibilities of people i.e. 'who does what'.

Employers

- ensure safe systems of work, safe plant and equipment, anything required for safety (e.g. PPE), access and egress
- ensure competent advice on health and safety matters
- obtain current Employers' Liability Insurance and display the certificate
- compile a health and safety policy and ensure that an adequate health and safety management system is in place
- ensure that risk assessments of all work activities are undertaken and any required controls are put in place

- provide the workforce with health and safety information and training
- provide adequate welfare facilities
- consult workforce on health and safety issues
- report and investigate some accidents, diseases and dangerous occurrences
- display prominently the health and safety law poster (or supply appropriate leaflet)

Directors

- health and safety arrangements are properly resourced
- competent health and safety advice is obtained
- regular reports are received on health and safety performance
- any new amended health and safety legislation is implemented
- risk assessments are undertaken
- there are regular audits of health and safety management systems and risk control measures
- and there is adequate consultation with employees on health and safety issues
- managing directors/chief executives, line managers and supervisors play key roles in ensuring that the health and safety policy is delivered and monitored

Safety advisor / competent person

- report directly to a senior management on matters of policy
- keep up to date with technological advances and legislative changes
- advice on establishment of health and safety, maintenance and accident investigation procedures

- provide liaison with external agencies, such as the HSE, fire authorities, contractors, insurance companies and the public
- participate in health and safety activities
- intervene in unsafe acts and conditions

Managers / supervisors

- area of responsibility is adequately controlled and supervised
- set a good example
- develop, understand and communicate Safe Systems of Work and Risk Assessments
- ensure health and safety performance is monitored
- deal with unsafe acts and conditions
- report to senior mangers
- investigate accidents and incidents
- ensure workers are trained, coached and mentored
- provide mentoring

Controllers of premises

- the safety of persons who are not their employees but use non-domestic premises made available to them as a place of work or as a place where they may use plant or substances provided for their use.
- the provision of ensuring safe access and egress to and from premises
- the maintenance or repair of any premises
- the safety and absence of risks to persons health arising from plant or substances

Employees

- follow Safe Systems of Work and procedures laid down by the organisation

- cooperate with managers and supervisors
- take care of themselves and others
- don't misuse or interfere with equipment and use as per training provided by employer
- report unsafe acts, conditions and significant uncontrolled hazards
- participate in development of Safe Systems of Work, procedures and Risk Assessments
- participate in specific duties e.g. first aider
- wear PPE provided by employer

Self employed

- whilst working at the clients site, shall take reasonable care of themselves and others
- cooperate with the employer and local site rules
- bring to the attention of their employer any shortcomings of those arrangements.
- not to intentionally, recklessly interfere with anything that has been provided in the interests of safety
- use equipment provided by the employer for safety

Note - If working alone, the self- employed also have specific duties e.g. reporting accidents - RIDDOR

Section 2: Culture

In this section:

1. Definition of culture
2. Influences on culture
3. Psychological factors
4. Effect of culture on performance
5. Improving culture

Learning Outcomes

Explain the concept of health and safety culture and its significance in the management of health and safety in an organisation

Safety culture - definition

The HSE define **safety culture** as:

- the product of individual and group values, attitudes, perceptions, competencies and patterns of behaviour that determine the commitment to, and the style and proficiency of, an organisation's health and safety management.

Commitment of management is the most important factor and will be enhanced by:

- visible management
- effective communication
- active employee participation
- effective health and safety training

Influences on culture

Internal influences on culture

- management commitment / effective communication
- production/service demands
- lack of investment / resources / management systems
- employee involvement
- zero tolerance to breaches of procedures
- blame culture / peer pressure
- acceptable behaviour
- worker moral

- retention of staff
- balance of health and safety over production goals
- effective supervision
- shared values
- competence / training / support of management
- employee representation
- adequate training and refresher training
- change in management structure / premises / environment
- job security

External influences culture

- expectations of society
- legislation and enforcement
- insurance companies
- stakeholders / interested parties
- local authorities
- HSE visits
- media
- company reputation
- pressure groups
- Trade Unions
- state of the economy
- commercial stakeholders
- external agencies e.g. fire service

Psychological factors

There are THREE factors that affect performance:

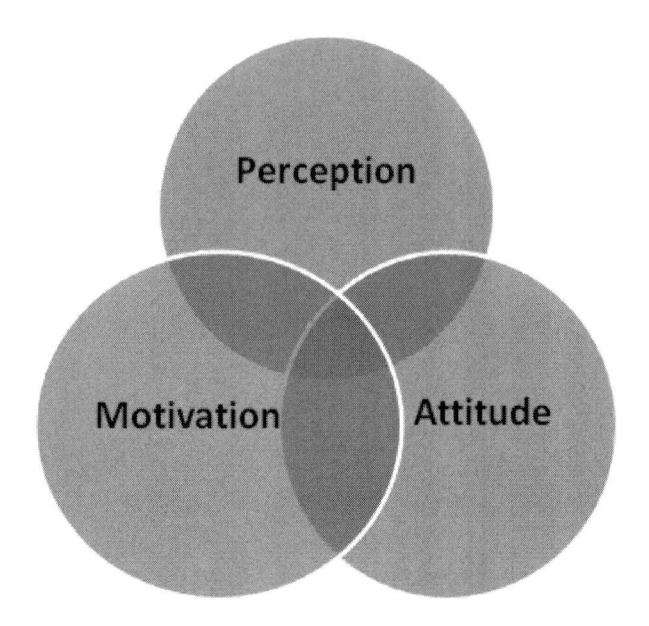

The THREE psychological factors that affect performance

Perception
The way in which a person believes or understands information supplied or a situation

Motivation
The driving force behind the why a person acts or is stimulated to act

Attitude
The tendency to behave in a particular way in a given situation, influenced by social background and peer pressure

Effect of culture on performance

All successes regarding health and safety are measured against pre-determined standards, and 'stem' from the policy.

Performance indicators can be used to target areas of deficiencies, non-compliance or improvement requirements.

Improving Culture

Culture can be improved by:

- visible management
- by improved or more effective communication processes
- active employee participation
- effective health and safety training

Consultation with employees

The Health and Safety (Consultation with Employees) Regulations 1996, identify the health and safety matters on which employers have a duty to consult with their employees:

- introduction of anything that may affect the health and safety of employees, such as new equipment or PPE
- arrangements for appointing competent persons
- health and safety documentation the employer has to provide employees e.g. evacuation procedures

Section 3: Human factors and influencing behaviour

In this section:

1. The three influencing factors
2. Human failure
3. Influencing behaviour

Learning Outcomes

- Outline the human factors which influence behaviour at work in a way that can affect health and safety
- Explain how health and safety behaviour at work can be improved

The three influencing factors

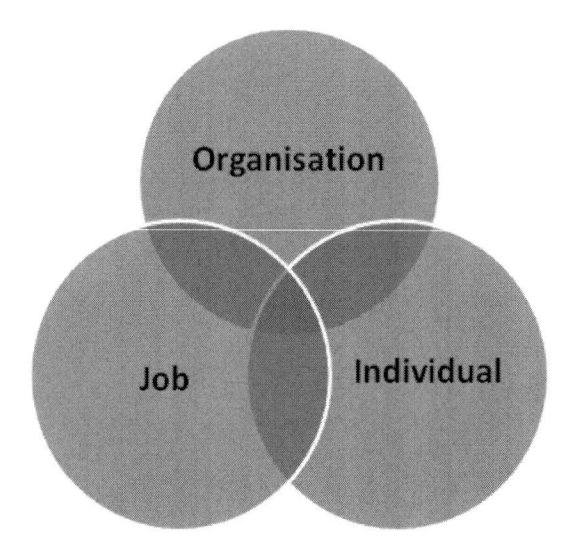

The THREE influencing factors that affect behaviour

Organisational factors - a few considerations

- must have a positive health and safety culture
- manage health and safety by providing leadership and involvement of senior managers
- motivate the workforce to improve health and safety performance
- measure health and safety performance

Job factors - a few considerations

- recognise possibility of human error
- good ergonomics, equipment design and layout of workstation
- clear job descriptions
- safe system of work and operating procedures
- job rotation and / or regular breaks
- provision of correct tools
- effective training schedule and good communication

Personal factors - a few considerations

- self-interest - e.g. effect of bonus system
- position in the team
- acknowledgement by management of good work initiatives
- hearing and/ or memory loss
- experience and competence
- an individual's personality and attitude
- individual's language skills e.g. a person may not understand or speak English
- training undertaken and information given
- effect of shift working - e.g. night working
- health (physical and mental)

Human failure

Human Failure is the failure of an individual to behave in the expected manner OR when someone has deviated from the expected manner.

When someone 'fails' they have not carried out a task correctly.

There are TWO basic categories of Human Failure; Human Error (Slips/Lapses or Mistakes) or Violations:

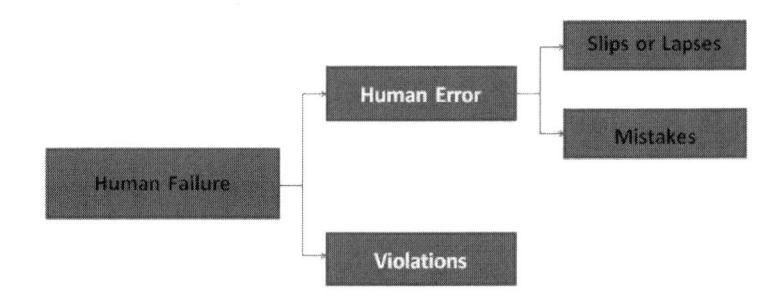

Human Error
Slips / Lapses

- failure to carry out particular actions that form part of a working procedure

Mistakes

- **rule-based** - a rule or procedure is applied or remembered incorrectly or
- **knowledge-based** - well tried methods or calculation rules are applied incorrectly

Violations
- **routine** - the breaking of a safety rule or procedure is the normal way of working

- **situational** - job pressures at a particular time make rule compliance difficult
- **exceptional** - a safety rule is broken to perform a new task

Influencing behaviour

Improving human behaviour is extremely difficult to achieve, especially if the culture of the organisation is weak and not driven from the senior management team.

In order to achieve stated objectives, the following factors need considering:

- recruiting only competent personnel
- the commitment from senior management
- the provision of effective and appropriate training and inductions
- management setting standards and 'leading by example'
- a good level of supervision
- communication and consultation with the workforce

Section 4: How to improve behaviour

In this section:

1. Securing commitment
2. Competent persons
3. Effective communication
4. Training

Learning Outcomes

Outline how to improve behaviour within an organisation

Securing commitment

In order to demonstrate commitment to the health and safety of the workforce, the management must have in place a system which includes the following factors and includes:

- a strong and robust management system
- senior management set a good example showing effective leadership
- health and safety targets are set for each departmental manager
- management have been provided with suitable health and safety management training
- adequate resources have been provided for each and every activity
- the individual performance measurement of targets and KPIs
- the processes of appraisals and assessments
- senior management of good standards and performance

Competent persons

A person is regarded as competent when they can demonstrate:

- sufficient skills, knowledge and experience to perform a task, as well as
- appropriate attitude, behaviour and motivation to perform the task

The level of competence depends on the complexity of the situation / task People need to be competent for the following reasons:

- it is a legal requirement e.g. Management of Health and Safety at Work Regulations

- improves performance
- safety culture is improved
- fewer accidents and incidents

Effective communication

Communication is the imparting or exchanging of information by speaking, writing, or using some other medium. There are essential TWO types of communication:

- **One-way communication** is when the receiver cannot respond to a message.
- **Two-way communication** is when the receiver can respond to a message. This allows confirmation the message has been both received and understood.

Effective communication means:

- all people (staff, contractors, visitors etc.) understand their roles and responsibilities, e.g. tasks are understood and work undertaken safely

- staff are motivated and there are business improvements and losses are reduced e.g. fewer accidents

Types of communication

There are THREE categories of communication:

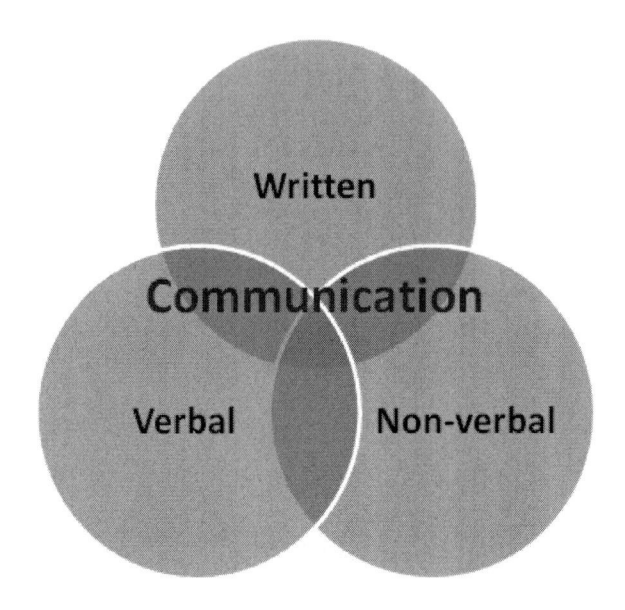

- **verbal or oral** (by mouth) - e.g. conversations, telephone
- **written** - e.g. memos, emails, meeting minutes, data sheets
- **non-verbal (graphic / visual)** - e.g. safety signs, posters, charts merits and limitations of different methods of communication

Methods of communication

The following is a non-exhaustive list of communication methods:

- formal lecture, training courses and on-the job training
- tool box talks and one-to-one discussions e-learning
- use of notice boards
- signs and signals e.g. sirens and bells

- books, CDs, videos
- meetings e.g. safety committee meetings
- safe systems of work / procedures e.g. Permit to Work

Barriers to communication

- language and dialect
- acronyms and jargon
- physical disability e.g. person is hard of hearing
- mental disabilities e.g. person cannot read
- attitudes and perception of workers and supervisors

Safety propaganda / messages

For safety propaganda or messages to be effective, it must have:
- a simple understandable message
- a positive believable message
- an appealing format that will motivate the recipient

Types of communication

The following communication systems are frequently used within an organisation:

- files, videos
- posters
- tool box talks
- memos
- worker handbooks
- cooperation and consultation with workforce
- meetings e.g. safety committee meeting
- worker feedback processes e.g. suggestion box

Training

Training is a systematic development of attitudes, knowledge and skills to perform adequately a task or job. The provision of training is a statutory requirement of an employer, mandated by the Health and Safety at Work etc. Act 1974 and numerous Regulations.

Employers' responsibilities to provide training

All responsible employers should:

- analyse the content of the job and the performance standards required
- be aware of the knowledge, experience and skill that will be required
- have a system in place to evaluate and assess an individual's present competence
- understand and implement various forms of training
- have a system in place to effectively evaluate the training provided
- have a system in place to monitor the effectiveness of any training provided
- identify specific hazards and risks and provide written instructions for machine operation (start, stop, running etc.)
- provide easily accessible information which is comprehensible and easily understood
- ensure supervisors and managers assess and record competence

Training review

Training must be reviewed when:

- a person changes their job

- there are process changes
- there is new or changed legislation
- there is an introduction of new technology
- a safe systems or processes mandate e.g. after a specific time scale

Types of training

Training can be categorised as:

- induction
- to meet competence levels
- maintaining competence levels
- when there are changes in operation, machines, technology etc.
- refresher training to 'remind' or 'reinforce' a message or process or specific safe systems

Induction training review

After the appointment of an employee, induction training is required to ensure that the person is safe and free from the hazards or dangers associated with that specific site.

Additional training and bespoke training will be provided at suitable times during the individuals' employment and/or career such as new or increased risks and refresher training.

Initial induction training would include the following areas:

- the health and safety policy and safe systems of work provided for the activities
- how to recognise and report unsafe conditions and uncontrolled hazards
- emergency procedures e.g. fire, bomb
- the location of the first aid station/box and medical room

- the supervisor in charge and safety (Trades' Union) representative
- accident reporting procedures
- location of the welfare facilities and rest rooms
- appropriate personal protective equipment requirements
- specific hazards e.g. fork truck movements
- safe walkways or pedestrian routes and no-go areas
- machinery pre-use equipment checks

Section 5: Emergency procedures

In this section:

1. Importance of developing procedures
2. Elements of emergency procedures

Learning Outcomes

Outline the need for emergency procedures and the arrangements for contacting emergency services

Importance of developing emergency procedures

It is important to develop emergency procedures because:

- it is legal requirement
- staff / visitors etc. need to be aware of what to do in an emergency and recognise the alarm
- essential to contain / mitigate effects / protect resources and the environment
- allows allocation of responsibilities e.g. fire warden
- it ensures emergency services are briefed
- ensures business continuity

- it meets the needs of specific groups e.g. disabled workers

When are emergency procedures required?

Emergency procedures are required when there is a possibility of a major accident or incident e.g.

- fire
- major transport incidents
- potential for significant explosion
- bomb or terrorist threat
- significant release of toxic gas / flammable liquid / hazardous substance
- natural disaster e.g. flood

Elements of emergency procedures

The following are elements of an emergency procedure:

- details of possible emergency, major accident or incident
- notices e.g. fire procedures (including testing)
- drills and evacuation procedures
- assembly and roll call arrangements
- arrangements for contacting emergency and rescue services
- provision of information for emergency services
- internal emergency organisation e.g. control of spillages and clean-up arrangements
- media and publicity arrangements
- business continuity arrangements
- consideration of persons with disability e.g. wheel chair bound persons

Section 6: Provision of first aid

In this section:

1. What is first aid?
2. First aid risk assessment
3. First aider provision
4. First aid facilities

Learning Outcomes

Outline the requirement for first aid in the workplace

What is first aid?

First aid is help given to a sick or injured person until full medical treatment is available.

Aim - to preserve life

Objectives

- prevent illness or injury from becoming worse
- relieve pain, if possible
- promote recovery
- protect the unconscious
- to reassure the injured person until medical help arrives

What to do if someone is injured

- secure scene
- call for help
- provide emergency assistance / first aid - if appropriate and qualified

- wait with the injured person until help arrives and reassure

First aid risk assessment

To undertake a first aid a risk assessment the following will need to be considered:

- number of people on site
- ratio of staff to visitors e.g. shop has many visitors
- specific hazards in the work place e.g. hazardous substance
- layout of site
- number of sites
- proximity of local medical facilities e.g. hospital
- competence of staff
- number of people with special needs e.g. disability, pregnancy, nursing mothers
- age and fitness of workforce

First aiders - numbers and type

The following are general classifications for the considerations of the numbers of first aiders:

Low Hazardous environment e.g. offices, shops, libraries would require:

- first aid requirements in a Low risk environment (less than 25 persons) could be covered by an appointed person. (Someone to call the emergency services and take care of the casualty)

Low risk environments e.g. between 25 - 50 persons

- at least 1 first aider trained in Emergency First Aid at Work (EFAW)
- first aid requirements in a Low risk environment (more than 50 persons)
- would normally be covered by at least one first aid trained person in First Aid at Work (FAW) and for every 100 or part thereof.

Higher risk environments e.g. engineering, machinery, plant, warehousing, construction and chemical production etc. should be covered by:

- less than 5 employees – at least 1 appointed person
- between 5 -50 employees – at least 1 first aider trained in EFAW or FAW, dependent upon the type of injuries that may occur
- more than 50 employees – at least 1 first aider trained in FAW for every 50 employed or part thereof.

Provision of first aid facilities

When considering first aid facilities the following will need to be considered:

- number of people with special needs
- adequate quantity of first aid boxes and located in close proximity to high risk areas
- all first aid boxes are to be managed and ensure regular checks of contents are undertaken
- contents of the first aid facilities (e.g. boxes) and replenished as required
- consideration of coverage in relation to shift work and geographical location

Chapter 4 - Health and Safety Management Systems Planning

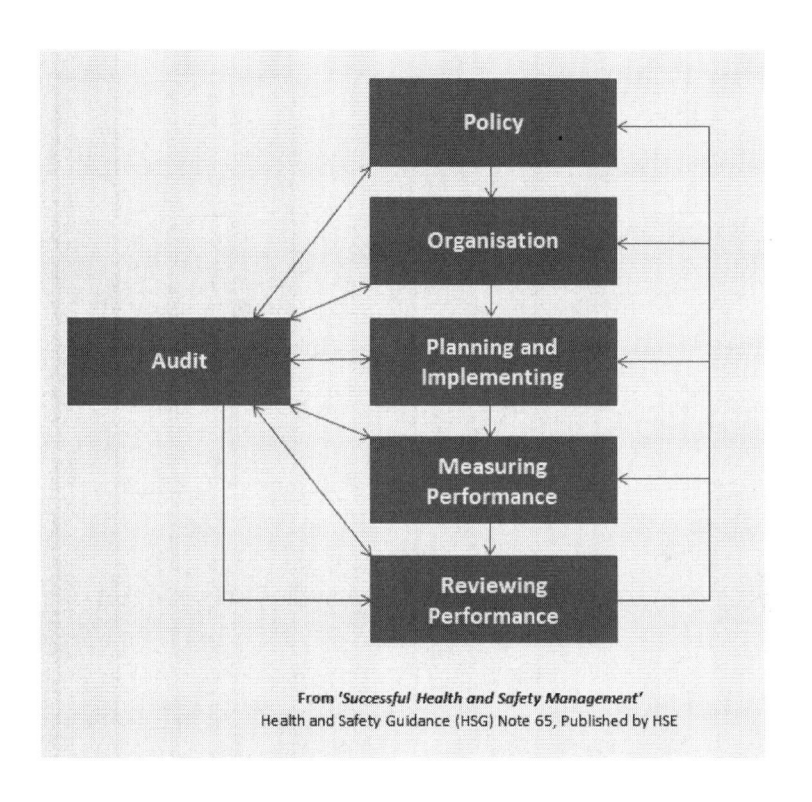

From *'Successful Health and Safety Management'*
Health and Safety Guidance (HSG) Note 65, Published by HSE

Section 1: Importance of planning

In this section:

1. Why planning is important
2. Setting objectives
3. Setting targets

Learning Outcomes

- Explain the importance of planning in the context of health and safety management systems

Why planning is important

It is essential to plan for Health and Safety for the following reasons:

- it is a legal requirement (Management of Health and Safety at Work Regulations 1999)
- ensures effective systems are in place for control, measuring and reviewing of preventative and proactive health and safety measures
- increases safety culture and staff moral
- ensures cost effectiveness - saves time, money and effort
- involves workforce in decision making, hence better risk management
- provides security and organisation to the company
- helps integrate and link all of the organization's functional departments

Setting objectives

In setting objectives the following need careful consideration:

- who is going to set the objectives – director, manager, supervisor?
- they need to be documented and set each functional level
- there needs to be a consideration of legal and other requirements
- specific hazards and risks
- financial, operational, and business requirements must be considered
- consultation to take place with interested parties e.g. employees, trades' union representatives
- objectives need to be SMART; Specific, Measurable, Achievable, Reasonable, Time bound objectives

Why set objectives?

- legal requirement e.g. Management of Health and Safety at work Regulations
- corporate requirement and shows management commitment. Often mandated within health and safety policy statement
- useful in measuring performance and something to aim for i.e. shows direction
- allows for benchmarking - internal and external

Setting targets

It is important to set objectives but they must be measurable. All targets must be **SMART**; Specific, Measurable, Achievable, Realistic and Timed.

Examples of targets:

- specific reduction in accidents, incidents and near misses. Some companies go for ZERO accidents as a goal. To have it as a target can cause problems as very few

companies have zero accidents, therefore the company could be setting an unrealistic target
- inspection and audit scores reduced OR number of inspections undertaken
- improved accident / incident reporting
- reduced ill-health and absenteeism due to health and safety reasons
- successful training outcomes
- reduced insurance premiums and civil claims
- positive behavioural safety observations
- employee uptake of initiatives or suggestions

Section 2: Principles of risk assessment

In this section:

1. What is risk assessment
2. Hazard and risk
3. The risk assessment process
4. Competence of risk assessors
5. Special Cases and Vulnerable Groups

Learning Outcomes

Explain the principles and practice of risk assessment

What is risk assessment?

Risk assessment is a process whereby hazards are identified, risk assessed to identify controls that reduce the risk to an acceptable level.

Hazard and risk

Hazard - something with the potential to cause harm e.g. electricity, hazardous substance, excessive noise

Risk - chance of harm occurring which is a combination of Likelihood and Severity

The risk assessment process

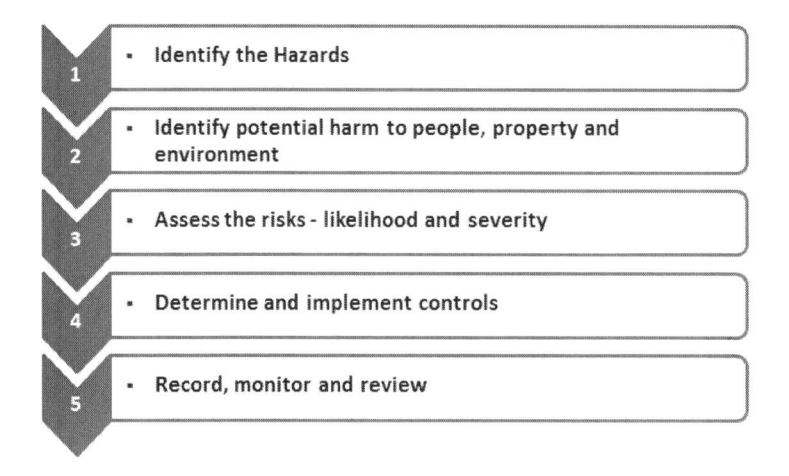

1. Identify the Hazards
2. Identify potential harm to people, property and environment
3. Assess the risks - likelihood and severity
4. Determine and implement controls
5. Record, monitor and review

1. Identify the Hazards

- e.g. identified during an inspection, comments from employees, update of ACoPs

2. Determine the people or property at risk

- employees, agency/ temporary workers, contractors, shift workers
- members of the public - visitors, customers, patients, students, children, elderly
- special groups - young persons, expectant or nursing mothers, workers with a disability, lone workers
- property, equipment that could be damaged

3. **Assess the risk level and determine the residual risk**

   - defined qualitatively or quantitatively
   - both occupational and organizational risk levels need to be considered
   - detail risk controls (existing and additional)

4. **Determine and implement the controls**

   - prioritisation of risk control
   - risks can be controlled by using the hierarchy of risk control (see later)

5. **Record, monitor and review**

   - only SIGNIFICANT risks need to be recorded
   - review if new/updated legislation, change in guidance
   - new information available on substances or process
   - changes to the workforce
   - introduction of trainees
   - an accident has occurred
   - after a pre-determined passage of time e.g. 3 years

Competence of risk assessors

A team approach is always recommended. Team *'requirements'* include:

- assessors need training in risk assessment process - i.e. they are competent
- leader should have health and safety experience or access to professional advice
- all need to know their own limitations - ability to know one's limitations is a measure of competence.

- team should include local line manager or supervisor
- person with detailed knowledge of the area or process
- at least one team member with report writing skills

Special cases and vulnerable groups

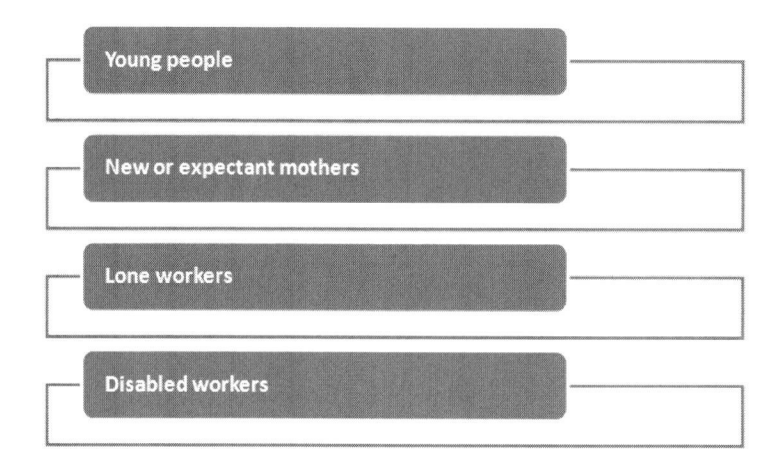

- Young people
- New or expectant mothers
- Lone workers
- Disabled workers

There are special cases for persons who may be exposed to some hazards which are outside the normal generic workplace. These could include:

- prison officers; traffic wardens; estate agents; district midwives; driving to or in a foreign country; security guards; lone workers

Young persons

Young persons will need special consideration because they can be:

- subject to peer pressure
- inexperienced in the working environment
- eager to please

- untrained of have a lack of knowledge about processes, hazards and risks
- unaware of generic activities

New or expectant mothers

There are restrictions on the type of work. In particular they should not:

- undertake excessive manual handling
- use certain chemical and biological agents e.g. teratogen (substance that can affect the unborn child)
- be exposed to ionising radiation, passive smoking, extreme temperature variations
- undertake prolonged standing, sitting or restricted movements
- be exposed to excessive stress and violent staff / visitors / customers

Disabled workers

Disability is any condition that can affect the person's ability to perform a task. There are a wide range of disabilities which can vary greatly. It may be necessary to have several individual risk assessments and a Personal Emergency Evacuation Plan (PEEP) for those that fall into this category e.g. wheelchair bound cannot evacuate premises if lifts are not used.

Reasonable adjustments for the specific disability e.g.

- allowing a person to work from home or working on the ground floor
- making provision for a Personal Emergency Evacuation Plan (PEEP) -
- changing or improving the work routine or layout

Lone workers

Lone workers are classed as a vulnerable group, due to the fact that a substantial part of their working time they are alone. It does not necessarily mean working away from site.

Such 'lone workers' could be:

- site security staff and cleaners
- persons working at a site but on their own for long periods unsupervised
- persons travelling abroad by themselves Special risk assessment could consider:
- fitness to work alone
- special training
- handling of equipment and substances alone
- periodic visits by supervisor
- communication e.g. regular mobile phone contact with base
- first aid arrangements
- emergency arrangements

Section 3: General principles of risk control

In this section:

1. General principles or risk reduction
2. Hierarchy of control
3. Suitable and sufficient risk control
4. Evaluating adequacy of controls

Learning Outcomes

Explain the general principles of control and a basic hierarchy of risk reduction measures

General principles for risk reduction

The principles of prevention are:

- avoid risks
- evaluate risks which cannot be avoided ~ adapt work to the individual
- adapt to technical changes
- replace dangerous items with less dangerous items
- develop an overall prevention policy
- give priority to collective measures (safe place strategy)
- ensure competence of employees to undertake the task

Hierarchy of control

The hierarchy of control is often known as **ERIC SP**:

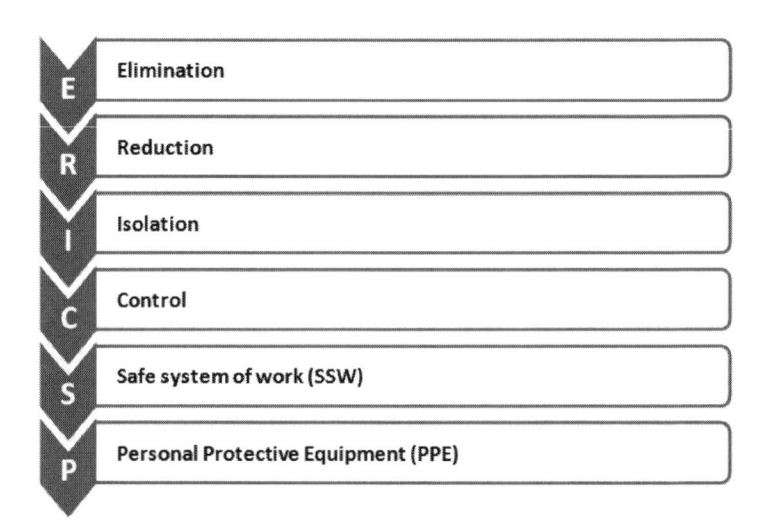

- **E** Elimination
- **R** Reduction
- **I** Isolation
- **C** Control
- **S** Safe system of work (SSW)
- **P** Personal Protective Equipment (PPE)

Suitable and sufficient risk control

A suitable and sufficient risk assessment will address the following:

- have all the steps in the risk assessment process been undertaken?
- is there a focus on prevention and organisational level solutions?
- has the provision for dealing with individual issues?
- is there commitment from all parties (senior management, employees and their representatives)?
- are there arrangements to identify those aspects of the work, organisation or environment that are known to be risk factors for work related stress?
- have workforce been involved - employees, supervisors etc.
- have questions been asked about regarding good and bad features of workplace conditions?
- have suggestions, advice and comments been received on potential solutions to problems?
- ensure people are been empowered to contribute and feel that their views are listened to and acted upon?
- have outcomes been communicated?
- has the assessment been documentation?

Evaluating adequacy of controls

The evaluation process is essential as it will ensure that risk assessments are adequate and controls are 'suitable and sufficient

Section 4: Sources of information

In this section:

1. Internal sources
2. External sources
3. Signs
4. HSE Poster

Learning Outcomes

Identify the key sources of health and safety information

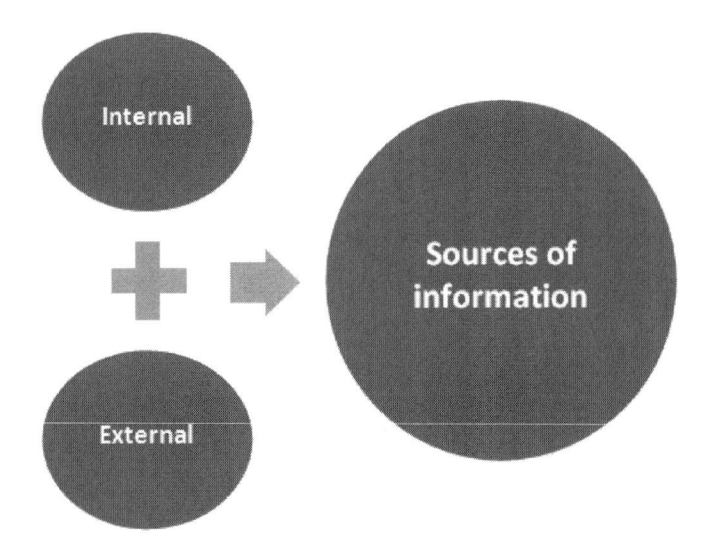

Internal sources

Internal sources of information could be:

- accident and ill-health records and investigation reports
- absentee records

- inspection and audit reports undertaken by the organization and by external organizations such as the HSE
- maintenance, risk assessment
- training records
- documents which provide information to workers
- any equipment examination or test reports
- committee meeting minutes
- other employees / contractors / visitors e.g. managers and supervisors
- safety officer / safety manager
- directors
- safety representatives

External sources

External sources to an organisation

- health and safety legislation
- Local Enforcing Authorities e.g. in the UK HSC
- publications such as Approved Codes of Practice, guidance documents, leaflets, journals, books and their website
- International European and British Standards
- health and safety magazines and journals e.g. IOSH
- information published by trade associations, employer organisations and trade unions
- specialist technical and legal publications
- information and data from manufacturers and suppliers / manufacturer's manuals / data sheets
- the Internet and encyclopedias

Signs

The following are the classifications of safety signs:

Type	Example
Prohibition White, round, red border, diagonal red line, black image	
Warning Yellow, triangular (usually), black border, black image	
Mandatory Blue, circular (usually), white symbol	
Safe condition Green, rectangular (usually), green, white symbol	
Fire Red, rectangular (usually), white symbol	

HSE Poster

The HSE poster **'WHAT YOU NEED TO KNOW'** must be displayed in a prominent place in ALL workplaces.

Section 5: Implementing a safe system of work

In this section:

1. Legal duties
2. What is a safe system of work?
3. Confined spaces

Learning Outcomes

Explain what factors should be considered when developing and implementing a safe system of work for general activities

Legal duties

The HASAWA requires employers to establish and maintain, so far as is reasonably practicable, systems which are safe and without risks.

What is a safe system of work?

Safe Systems of Work (sometimes called Method Statements) are formal systems for undertaking a task.

It is the employer's responsibility (duty) to provide safe systems of work, however, they must be produced and written by competent persons.

In developing a Safe System of Work it is important to remember:

- the importance of worker involvement in their development
- importance and relevance of written procedures
- clearly written procedures that can be understood by the reader. They may have to be in different languages!
- there is a distinction between technical, procedural and behavioural controls
- it is necessary to analyse tasks and undertake a formal risk assessment to determine effective controls
- provide the necessary information, instruction and training in the operation of the system and ensure competence of operators of the system
- supervise the process

- monitor the system

Confined spaces

A confined space can be defined as any place, including any chamber, tank, vat, silo, pit, trench, pipe, sewer, flue, well or other similar space in which, by virtue of its enclosed nature, there arises a reasonably foreseeable specified risk.

Typical hazards

- lack of oxygen and asphyxiation / poor ventilation / presence of fumes or gases
- poor means of access and escape
- drowning / claustrophobia
- electrical equipment (needs to be flameproof)
- presence of dust (e.g. silos)
- heat and high temperatures ~ fire and/or explosion
- poor or artificial lighting
- restricted movement
- lifting and carrying in restricted area

Controls

The following controls could be part of a Safe System of Work, but obviously depends on circumstances

- Permit-to-Work (PTW)
- formal risk assessment
- hazard identification
- training and information for all workers entering the confined space
- competence of people entering confined space
- emergency arrangements in place and emergency training
- restricted entry / cordon off area
- communication - outside / inside

- second person on stand-by
- forced ventilation
- gas testing (hazardous substances and oxygen) and monitoring
- appropriate PPE e.g. harness / breathing apparatus
- isolation of services e.g. Certificate of Isolation (CoI) of inlet pipes into tank

Section 6: Permit to Work (PTW)

In this section:

1. When is a PTW needed?
2. Elements of a PTW
3. Specific PTW

Learning Outcomes

Explain the role and function of a Permit To Work system (PTW)

When is a PTW needed?

A 'Permit to Work' is a formal, written, permission to undertake potentially hazardous activities. The permit details the work to be done and the precautions to be taken and maybe part of a Safe System of Work. It is NOT a safe system of work

Required for any specific high risk activity, decided by the organisation e.g.:

- welding
- hot works
- confined space work

- working at height (significant height)
- specialist maintenance activities
- working on high pressure systems
- buried services
- working under or passing under overhead power lines
- excavations close to adjacent buildings or structures / or deep excavations
- certain types of electrical work e.g. 'working live'
- use of significant amounts of flammable liquids

Elements of a PTW

The following should be present on all PTWs:

- permit title
- reference number
- job location
- plant identification
- description of work to be done and its limitations and time duration
- hazard identification
- precautions necessary
- Personal Protective Equipment, specialist tools or equipment
- acceptance (signature date and time)
- extension (signature extension date and time i.e. valid for how long)
- handback (signature date and time)
- cancellation (signature date and time)

A PTW should only last 1 shift, and only be extended ONCE. If PTWs are left 'open' between shifts errors can occur.

Specific PTW

Permit to Work certificates are often modified for specific situations e.g.:

- working at height (Significant or presenting specific high risk activities)
- entry into confined spaces
- hot work - so called because it produces ignition sources or large amounts of heat e.g. welding, grinding

Chapter 5 - Health and Safety Management Systems Measuring, Review and Auditing

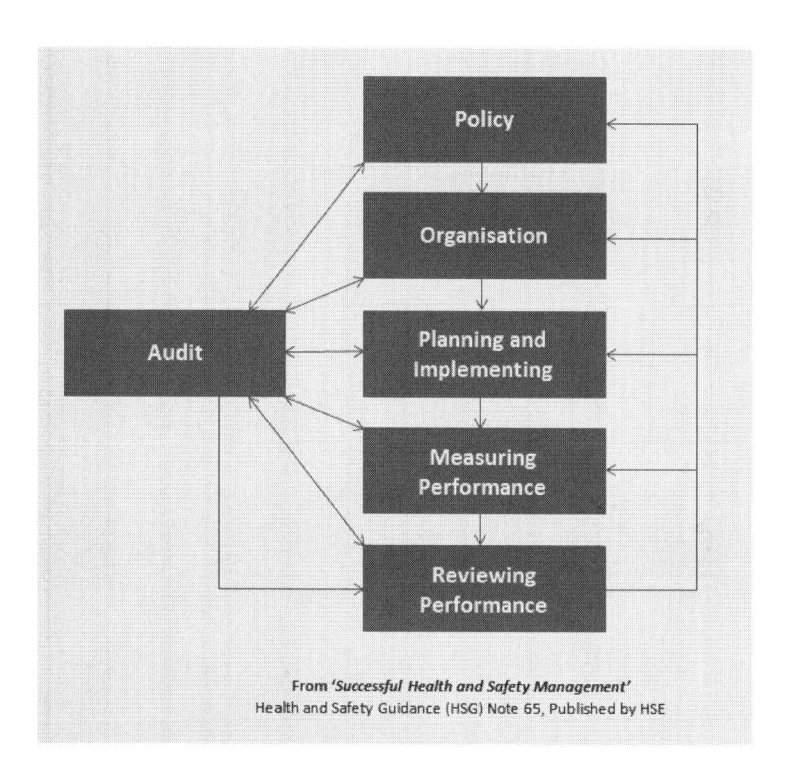

From *Successful Health and Safety Management*'
Health and Safety Guidance (HSG) Note 65, Published by HSE

Section 1: Active and reactive monitoring

In this section:

1. Principles of active and reactive monitoring
2. Why monitor?
3. Types of monitoring

Learning Outcomes

Outline the principles, purpose and role of active and reactive monitoring

Principles for monitoring

Monitoring can be summarised into two categories:

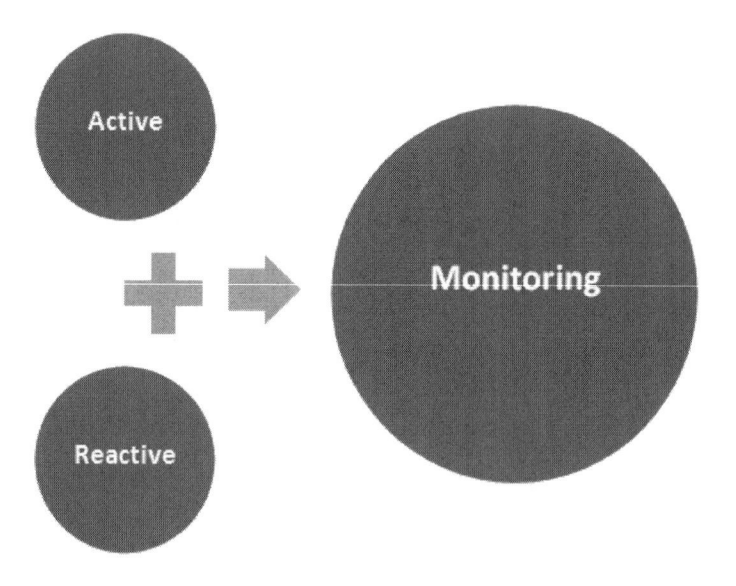

- **Active monitoring** (sometimes called Pro-active Monitoring) will consider:

- the direct observation of workers e.g. safe / unsafe acts, behavioural observations
- meeting with management and workers to discuss issues
- checking documents e.g. maintenance records, near miss reports, insurance reports
- undertaking workplace inspections, sampling, surveys, tours and audits
- benchmarking - internal and external, against recognised standards

- **Reactive monitoring** (taking action after a problem occurs) will consider:
- accident and ill-health reports
- procedures following dangerous occurrences, property damage or near miss reports
- compensation claims, litigation or advice comments for enforcing authorities
- complaints from the workforce (employees, managers, supervisors etc.), members of the public or third parties e.g. insurance company
- procedures following enforcement reports and notices
- risk assessments following the discovery of additional hazards

Why monitor?

Organisations need to measure what they are doing to implement their health and safety policy to assess how well they are

- meeting the aims and objectives of the policy
- controlling risks
- developing a positive health and safety culture
- improving performance

Types of monitoring

There are various types of monitoring techniques. They include:

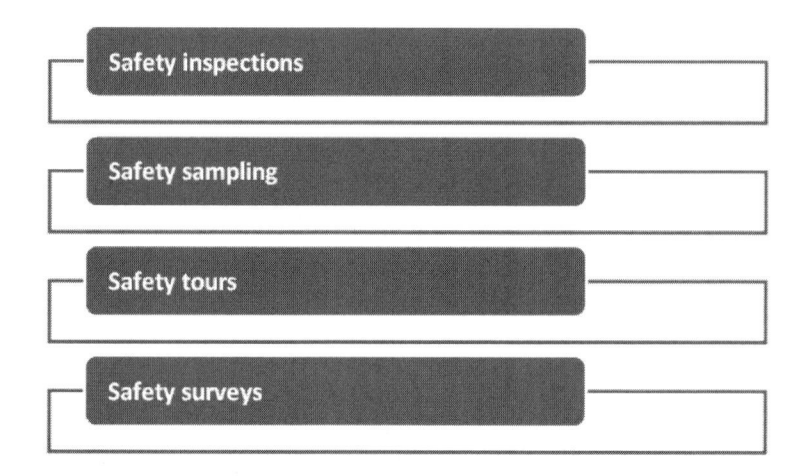

- Safety inspections
- Safety sampling
- Safety tours
- Safety surveys

Safety inspections

Detailed check, often using a checklist, of the workplace to identify non-compliance to standards and identify uncontrolled hazards. They should cover:

- physical inspection of premises (e.g. access/egress, housekeeping)
- plant, equipment and substances (e.g. machine guarding, tools, ventilation)
- procedures in place (e.g. safe systems of work, risk assessments, use of personal protective equipment)
- the workforce (e.g. training, information, supervision, health surveillance) When conducting inspections consideration needs to be given to:
- the competence of the inspectors and who will be an inspector e.g. safety representative, supervisor

- who will undertake an inspection e.g. safety or employee representatives, supervisors, safety officer
- the frequency of inspections e.g. daily, weekly, monthly
- the response to the inspection report - actions for improvement
- the use of objective inspection standards

Safety sampling

Safety Sampling is the checking for safety defects in a selected area of the workplace (e.g. all fire extinguishers).

Often uses a pre-determined checklist to address issues that are identified as needing attention.

Safety tours

Safety tours are a 'tour' of a work area in the workplace by a team led by a senior manager. Good safety tours:

- the aim is to show senior management commitment for health and safety and the improvement of standards
- they do not use a pre-determined checklist
- a report produced highlighting good practice and areas of improvement
- a pre-arranged, starts with an informal meeting to discuss tour, after tour meeting to discuss / make recommendations
- most important to raise awareness and move safety up the agenda

Safety surveys

Safety surveys are a detailed inspection of a particular workplace activity throughout an organisation e.g. fire and emergency procedures, implementation and use of the Permit to Work (PTW)

Section 2: Health and safety auditing

In this section:

1. What is a health and safety audit?
2. Scope and purpose
3. Undertaking an audit
4. Internal and external auditing

Learning Outcomes

Explain the purpose of, and procedures for, a health and safety auditing

What is a health and safety audit?

A Health and Safety Audit is an in-depth review of the Safety Management System / Health and Safety Policy and its implementation. It can determine the levels of compliance through a rigorous and systematic examination which have been set and measured against agreed standards in requirements of legislation and best practice.

Scope of a health and safety audit

The scope or depth of the audit will depend upon the inherent hazards associated with the site. There may not be a full system audit, in which case, it will look specific elements of the Health and Safety Management System

Specific areas often included in the audit are:

- accident reporting and incident data

- emergency evacuation procedures
- fire prevention
- competence and training

Undertaking the audit

The Audit should take place at regular intervals (e.g. yearly) and will be undertaken by a combination of

- interviews
- document reviews
- observations of behaviours

Consideration also needs to be given to:

- production of a report and action plans
- conformance / non-conformance to standards
- competence of auditors. The following will need consideration:
- interview skills
- recording skills and process
- ability to review documents
- to be impartial
- ability to communicate with interviewees
- knowledge of processes and procedures
- use of pre-determined questions with scoring system

Internal vs external auditing

	Advantages	Dis-advantages
Internal Audits	<ul><li>easy to arrange</li><li>the auditor has knowledge of the processes</li><li>familiar with the local environment</li><li>lower in terms of time and cost</li><li>understands and implements industry standards</li></ul>	<ul><li>person may not be competent in auditing skills</li><li>subject to pressure from Peers or Senior Management</li><li>not up to date with current standards or legislation</li><li>auditor may be responsible for implementing the changes required</li><li>the auditor may assume processes are in order</li><li>not taken seriously by management</li><li>not all areas of site audited due to time constraints</li><li>may be bias towards the site/department</li></ul>

	Advantages	Dis-advantages
External Audits	<ul><li>impartial to the activities and the industry standards</li><li>a wide range of different types of work</li><li>maybe able to offer solutions to unsolvable issues or problems</li><li>not inhibited to criticism</li><li>auditing without bias</li><li>normally no internal relationship with person being audited</li></ul>	<ul><li>can be difficult to arrange</li><li>need to discuss the scope and depth</li><li>more expensive</li><li>lack of cooperation with the auditor</li><li>auditor needs to ask questions</li><li>interviews a wide range of staff</li><li>formal methods of auditing used</li><li>can be intimidating to the auditee</li><li>individuals may not provide the accurate and honest information</li></ul>

Competence of auditors

Auditing person or team has been selected from competent persons internally or externally such as:

- Health and Safety Practitioner
- auditing skills
- report writing and presentation skills
- knowledge of systems and processes
- specialist knowledge e.g. chemists or radiation protection advisors or supervisors, occupational nurse, quality Assurance or environmentalists

Planning the audit

- notification has been given in writing and that contact has been made with the auditee
- the lead auditor has established an audit plan
- sufficient time to locate and make available any information or records requested or site specific documents (risk assessment, policy)
- company data has been reviewed e.g. accident and incidence rates
- a proposed audit schedule, dates and timetable
- details of the audit team have been provided
- interviews have been inserted into diaries of key members of management
- methods of feedback outlined, e.g. presentation, hard copies, video conferencing etc.
- pre-meeting arranged to explain the specific objectives of the process and to provide answers to any issues or queries

Sources of information for the audit

- Health and Safety Policy / safety management system

- company training records
- emergency procedures
- risk assessments
- accident and incident reports
- equipment pre-use inspection records
- health surveillance records e.g. noise surveys
- maintenance procedures and reports
- trend analysis
- health and safety committee meeting reports
- action planning for safety related issues
- previous audit reports

Interviewing - Audits

When conducting interviews the following will need consideration:

- carry out interviews during normal working hours and establish the person's specific role or job function
- establish a rapport with the interviewee and put the person at ease during questioning
- explain the purpose and role of the auditing process
- avoid any potential leading question or suggestion
- read back to the interviewee, review and summarise the main points
- briefly discuss the next steps that the audit will take
- thank the person for their cooperation, honesty, and being frank and open

Conclusions

Conclusions based upon the information gathered and analysed and make recommendations for improvement.

Report

A report and presentation should be detailed and presented to senior management team.

Section 3: Investigating accidents

In this section:

1. Accidents and incidents and why they occur
2. Investigation process
3. Immediate and root causes

Learning Outcomes

Explain the purpose of, and procedures for, investigating incidents (accidents, cases of work-related ill-health and other occurrences)

Why accidents and incidents occur

Two important definitions:

- an **accident** is an undesired event that causes harm
- an **incident** (or near miss) is an undesired event with the potential to cause harm

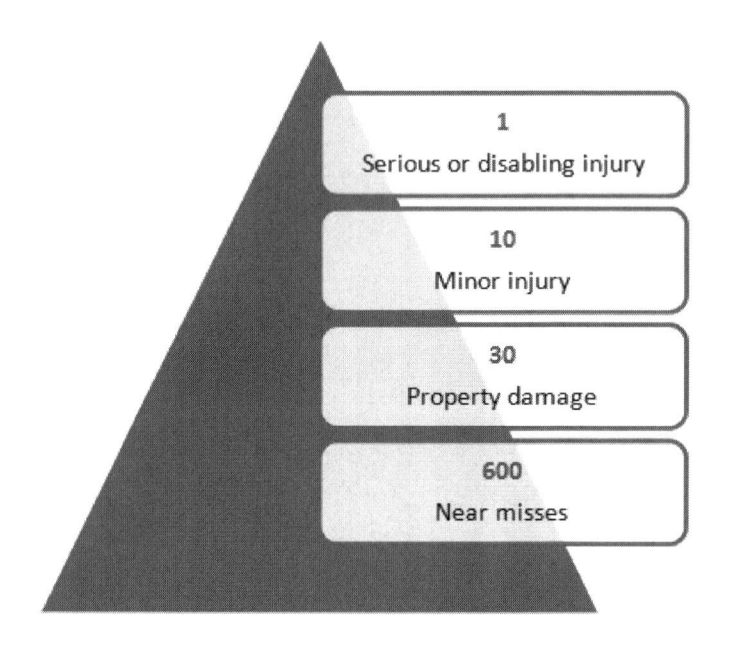

Accidents and incidents occur when barriers break down (or are not in place) therefore resulting in harm

Investigation process

The main aim of accident and incident investigation is to identify the immediate and root causes to prevent a recurrence. Other reasons include:

- it shows management commitment
- it is a legal requirement e.g. RIDDOR
- to identify failings in Risk Assessments, Safe Systems of Work, procedures etc.
- it encourages reporting
- to analysis of trends
- outcomes can be used to defend civil claims or legal proceedings

Investigation is a 4 stage process:

Step 1 – **Gathering** Information
Step 2 – **Analysing** information
Step 3 – **Determine** preventative solutions
Step 4 – **Implement** recommendations by the setting objectives

Step 1 – Gathering Information

The gathering of essential information will be necessary to fully understand the sequence of events leading up to the incident such as:

- where and when the incident occurred
- who was the injured person (if any) and who were the witnesses
- results of any interviews carried out - injured party and witnesses
- photographs, or drawings (hand sketches or Technical data) of the site
- workplace layout, size and configuration
- machinery, plant, or equipment involved
- should the investigation be carried out by internal or external staff
- weather conditions and time of year, e.g. winter or summer
- workplace environmental conditions e.g. lighting
- competence of people involved
- risk assessments, procedures and SSoW that were applicable to the accident or incident
- level of supervision

Step 2 – Analysing information

After gathering information, a reasonable understanding of what has occurred and an indication towards any management system failings will develop, including:

- immediate causes
- underlying and root causes
- human factors, errors and violations
- job/task factors
- organisational factors

Step 3 - determine preventative solutions

In order to prevent an incident reoccurrence, it is vital that suitable risk control measures are identified and effective solutions introduced as early as possible.

Preventative solutions and the revision of safety management systems would include:

- technical issues and controls (engineering controls that do not involve human interaction)
- procedures and safe systems of work
- human factors including behavioural controls

Step 4 – Implement by the setting objectives

In order to ensure that any solutions, preventative measures or recommendations introduced, a risk control action plan should be devised prioritising for both the short term and long term time periods.

The risk control action plan should in place using **SMART** objectives i.e. Specific, Measurable, Agreed, Realistic, and within a given Timescale.

This will be based upon the specific areas of concern and what issues need to be remedied or addressed immediately such as:

- which risk assessments / SSoW need to be reviewed?
- any incident trends that may need further investigation
- the requirements of additional training
- machinery, equipment and plant pre-use safety checks
- level of supervision and supervisory rotas
- training requirement

Immediate and root causes

Immediate causes

- An **unsafe act** - when an individual does something that is likely to cause harm
- An **unsafe condition** - when something is left in a state that is likely to cause harm
- Unsafe acts and unsafe conditions are the immediate causes and occur immediately prior to the accident or incident

Root causes

Although it is not possible to obtain a definitive definition of underlying and root causes, the following provide a generalised synopsis:

- **Underlying cause** - system or organisational failure or reason for the adverse event
- **Root cause** - initiating event or failing, often the result of management system failure

Examples of immediate, underlying and root causes. Consider the following accident

- person received electric shock from a bare wire on a 230V extension cable

Immediate cause (could be)	Bare electrical cable
Underlying causes (could be)	Lack of maintenance of equipment
	Visual inspection of operator
Root causes (could be)	Failure to identify requirement to regularly maintain equipment (general categorisation - preoccupied)
	Lack of competence of managers / supervisors (general categorisation - poor training)
	Little use of risk assessments to identify hazards and determine control measures (general categorisation - lack of risk assessment)

Section 4: Recording and reporting incidents

In this section:

1. Why record accidents and incidents
2. RIDDOR and types of incident

Learning Outcomes

Describe the legal and organisational requirements for recording and reporting incidents

Why record accidents and incidents

The following are reasons why it is important to record accidents and incidents:

- to comply with relevant legislation, ACoPs and guidance

- the early identification of any failings in the safety management systems
- informs an employer where improvements need to be made
- enables trends to be identified
- allows comparisons in performance measurement / benchmarking
- provides information in similar business to gain the competitive edge
- provides information as to what risk assessments or safe systems of work need to be reviewed
- information recorded can assist in deciding what to do to improve standards

RIDDOR

RIDDOR - Reporting of Injuries, Diseases and Dangerous Occurrences Regulations 2013

Employers and self-employed must keep a record of:

- any reportable death, injury, occupational disease or dangerous occurrence
- all occupational accidents and injuries that result in a worker being away from work or incapacitated for more than 7 consecutive days

What must be reported?

- deaths
- **major injuries** e.g. fracture (other than to fingers, thumbs and toes), amputation, loss of sight due to chemical in eye,
- over 7-day injuries
- specified occupational diseases

- **specified dangerous occurrences** e.g. the collapse, overturning or failure of load-bearing parts of lifts and lifting equipment; plant or equipment coming into contact with overhead power lines

How to report

- HSE website for e.g. person breaking their leg or collapse of a large scaffolding
- telephone (quickest possible means) e.g. death of person

Section 5: Review of health and safety performance

In this section:

1. Purpose of review
2. Undertaking a review
3. Records
4. Reporting and feedback processes

Learning Outcomes

Explain the purpose of, and procedures for, regular reviews of health and safety performance

Purpose of review

The purpose of a review is to determine if the Health and Safety Management System is working and whether it could be improved e.g.

- are the objects being met?
- is the whole system fit-for purpose and addressing issues in a logical way?

When should a review be undertaken?

- when there are significant organisational changes
- there have been changes in personnel and/or legislation
- introduction of new plant and equipment
- health and safety performance has fallen below the occupational group's benchmarks
- the monitoring of risk assessments and/or accident/incident investigations indicate that the health, policy is no longer totally effective

- enforcement action has been taken by the HSE or Local Authority
- a sufficient period of time has elapsed since the previous review
- request by third party e.g. insurance company

Undertaking a review

During the review the following needs to be considered:

- evaluations of compliance with applicable legal and organisational requirements
- accident and incident data, corrective and preventive actions
- inspections, surveys, tours and sampling
- absences and sickness
- quality assurance reports
- audits
- monitoring data/records/reports
- external communications and complaints
- results of participation and consultation
- objectives met
- actions from previous management reviews
- legal/good practice developments

Records

Records must be kept as they demonstrate continuous improvements and are a useful source of information when:

- carrying out future audits
- presentation to enforcing authorities
- presentation to interested parties e.g. Trade Unions Representatives, employees

Reporting and feedback processes

After completing a review it is essential to feedback to all interested parties e.g. directors, senior managers, employees etc.

This will enable the creation of action plans for continual improvement.

Chapter 6 - Workplace Hazards and Risk Control

Section 1: Health, welfare and work environment requirements

In this section:

1. Health and Welfare provisions
2. Temperature

Learning Outcomes

Outline the common health, welfare and work environment requirements in the workplace

Health and Welfare provisions

All workplaces should have the following welfare facilities:

- supply of drinking water
- washing facilities
- sanitary conveniences
- accommodation for clothing
- rest and eating facilities
- seating
- ventilation
- heating and lighting

Supply of drinking water

- adequate supply of 'wholesome' drinking water is readily available
- drinking water supplied through a tap should have suitable drinking vessels
- water that is not 'wholesome', labelled 'not suitable for drinking'

Washing facilities

Suitable and sufficient Washing facilities should be provided for all employees and be readily accessible. Special considerations to the nature of the work undertaken may include the provision of showers.

In all cases, there must be a supply of:

- clean, hot and cold running water
- soap or other form of cleaning agents along with towel or other means of drying
- adequately maintained; kept clean and ventilated;
- adequate lighting

Sanitary conveniences

Separate Sanitary Conveniences for both men and women, other that in a separate room, where the door can be secured from the inside. Other requirements include:

- suitable and sufficient for the numbers of persons employed
- readily available
- kept clean, well lit and ventilated

Dependent upon the nature of the working environment, personal clothing may not be suitable for the activities undertaken whilst at work. In this case:

- personal clothing not worn at work must be kept secure by the provision of suitable accommodation
- personal clothing worn at work, should be adequately stored when not in use, kept secure by the provision of suitable accommodation to avoid any health risks or damage

- drying facilities may be appropriate

Accommodation for changing clothing

- provided for employees where a person needs to change into some specialist clothing for safety reasons e.g. another room
- separate facilities or separate use of facilities for male and female
- be suitable and sufficient, readily accessible to workrooms and eating facilities (if provided) and should also be furnished with adequate seating arrangements

Rest facilities

- suitable and sufficient rest facilities readily e.g. small kitchenette or modified workplace
- where meals are regularly consumed in the workplace, suitable and sufficient facilities must be provided
- suitable rest facilities must be provided for nursing mothers or pregnant women
- suitable and sufficient numbers of tables and seats
- offices can be acceptable as rest facilities provided workers are not subject to excessive disturbance during rest periods
- should include a facility for preparing or obtaining hot drinks
- a means of heating workers own food e.g. microwave
- canteens can be used as rest facilities, but cannot be charged for entry or forced to purchase food

Seating

- suitable seats must be provided for workers who, from time to time or during rest periods, need to be seated.

- pregnant or nursing mothers should also have facilities available to lie down if required
- provision and maintenance of an adequate supply of fresh circulated air must be provided in every occupied workplace. In addition to this, a system to render harmless any airborne contaminants, e.g. dusts, fumes, vapours or gasses

Heating

- appropriate to aid physical comfort; identified or achieved through the initial environmental assessment

Not all work environments will be able to make adjustments to temperature e.g. oil installation platforms, ambient warehouse, laundry facilities, frozen food manufacturing, areas around ovens and kilns and steel and glassworks. In such circumstances:

- suitable provision must be made e.g. use of PPE (e.g. thermal clothing) or job rotation
- other factors to consider are individual capability, wind velocity, humidity and extremes of temperatures
- all places of work must be adequately lit
- natural light is best; however, too much natural light can be hazardous, therefore the following could be considered; blinds, anti-glare surfaces to furniture and screens, tinted window glazing and screens for computers
- considerations to the time of day, especially the winter months or working through the hours of darkness will pose a safety issue due to poor lighting.
- lighting assessments for workplace activities such as: emergency evacuation, vehicular movement, machinery operations,
- portable lighting can be used to increase the levels of light, e.g. carrying out maintenance

Temperature

Extremes of temperature

- extremes of temperature risk assessments for specific environments
- exposure to extremes of temperature need to be minimised and varies in different working environments e.g. in sunshine, furnaces, foundries, kilns, ovens, bakeries, laundries
- need to be monitored and managed accordingly

Hot and humid environments

- health effects include; heat syncope, rashes, heat exhaustion, heat cramps, heat stroke, fainting, and lack of concentration, lethargy, and unconsciousness

Some of the controls may include:

- individual capabilities and information, instruction, training and supervision
- environmental monitoring (the use of a hygrometer, thermometer)
- acclimatisation to the environment and adequate ventilation and provision of cold drinks and / or salt replacement drinks
- light and loose clothing
- job rotation

Cold and external environments

Health effects environment include; loss of concentration, reduced mobility, reduced dexterity, shivering, chilblains, frost bite, trench foot and hypothermia

Controls could include or be a combination of:

- recovery room (warm break away area)
- individual capabilities
- environmental monitoring (the use of a thermometer)
- information, instruction, training and supervision
- acclimatisation to the environment
- hot drinks
- manual activities (to raise the body temperature) need careful consideration
- PPE e.g. thermal clothing; undergarments; gloves, scarf's or hats; foot protection (thermal socks)
- job rotation

Section 2: Violence at work

In this section:

5. What is violence?
6. Risk factors
7. Control measures
8. Risk assessment

Learning Outcomes

Explain the risk factors and appropriate controls for violence at work

What is violence?

The term Violence does not just refer to the physical form of violence e.g. personal injury, through slap, kick, bruises, bloodied nose or broken bones, but also the psychological injuries through bullying and harassment.

Groups at risk include

There are working environments / employment situations that put workers at risk from violence such as:

- lone workers
- taxi drivers
- people representing authority e.g. court officials, doorman/women at a night club
- visiting midwifes, health visitors and doctors
- uniformed people in authority e.g. prison officers, police, security guards, traffic wardens
- care workers and hospital staff
- teaching staff and assistants

Non-physical violence

The psychological element of violence is much more difficult to evaluate because it's what is happening in the head, the heart and the emotional effects that is causing suffering to the person.

Factors relating to non-physical violence such as:

- the setting of unachievable targets or tasks
- publicly humiliating people
- dressing down
- whispering behind people's backs
- overlooking in promotion
- personal verbal attacks
- failing to include persons in social events
- purposely ostracising individuals through exclusion

Control Measures

Control measures to deal with the physical and non-physical elements would include:

- undertaking workplace assessments
- barriers and restricted access to areas
- security staff and security equipment e.g. CCTV, panic alarm
- staffing levels
- lone working policy and procedure
- incident reporting
- disciplinary measures
- confrontational training
- stress reduction techniques
- drugs and alcohol policy and controls
- specific issues for identified groups e.g. two members of staff if 'home' visiting if person being visited is aggressive, panic alarm for police
- ensure areas e.g. car parks are well lit

Dealing with incidents

- debrief the individual and encourage him/her to talk through and share their experience
- sign off from work providing sufficient time to recover from the ordeal
- provide counselling to victims and offer support
- consideration to a phased return to work
- access to legal advice in serious cases
- consider other workers and provide guidance to assist them in understanding what to do, should an event of violence occur and how to react appropriately.

Risk Assessment - Violence

The following need to be considered when undertaking a suitable risk assessment:

- identify vulnerable groups and numbers of people affected
- identify who might be harmed and how
- evaluate the risks be checking existing arrangements
- provide training to all workers to identify the early signs of violence
- provide information on past historical events
- zero tolerance policy regarding violence at work
- improve the forms and types of security required e.g. video cameras, coded digital-locks, panic alarms
- re-design workplace
- use of credit cards as opposed to cash
- having two workers on site in high risk areas
- arrange transport for persons who work during the hours of darkness
- removal of items that could be used as weapons

Section 3: Substance Misuse

In this section:

1. Risk factors
2. Control measures

Learning Outcomes

Explain the effects of substance misuse on health and safety at work and control measures to reduce such risks

Substance Misuse - Risk Factors

The risks to health and safety from the use of alcohol and drugs whilst at work are:

- reduced perception
- loss of hand-eye coordination
- overall state of health
- poor fatigue and lethargy
- stress and emotional effects
- poor attitude and increase in violent events
- road traffic accidents
- not adhering to site rules
- minor and major accidents

Control Measures

At induction, all workers will be provided with the standards that are mandated on all employees. Some of the requirements could include:

- documented and communicated policy and procedures
- entire workforce should be banned from being under the influence of alcohol and drugs whilst in the workplace
- providing opportunities to discuss alcohol and drug issues and their effects
- carrying out random alcohol and drug tests
- after an incident consider weather alcohol or drugs may have been a factor
- vehicle drivers tested after incidents

Section 4: Safe movement of people

In this section:

2. Hazards in the workplace
3. Control measures for specific environments / situations

Learning Outcomes

Explain the hazards and control measures for the safe movement of people in the workplace

Hazards in the workplace

Hazards due to movement of people include:

- issues relating to surfaces - slips, trips and falls on the same level
- issues relating to working at height
- moving vehicles
- flying or falling objects
- striking against fixed or stationary objects
- conditions and environments in which each hazard may arise e.g. weather

Slips trips and falls at same level - issues

- poorly maintained surfaces such as highly polished floors
- damaged floor tiles, carpets or mats
- pot holes in roads
- on-site debris and obstructions
- insecure ducting and insecure grate covers
- changes in levels of surface not marked
- damaged road surface e.g. due to heavy vehicle use

- slippery surfaces internal and external due to spillages of mud, silt, oils and fuels
- inappropriate footwear
- employees not taking care e.g. running on site
- ice and snow
- trailing cables

Falls from height - issues

- poorly or inadequately designed access or egress from a place of work, e.g. vehicle tail board, flat roof
- fragile roof, such as asbestos sheeted or composite roof panels
- no, or inadequate, edge protection, hand rails or barriers
- falling into unprotected trenches due to not being covered or fence protection provided

Coming into contact with moving vehicles - issues

- insufficient maneuvering or passing space
- congestion of traffic
- vehicles traversing across slopes
- poorly planned or defined traffic routes for pedestrian access and egress
- reversing vehicles into loading and unloading areas due to no banksman
- employees not following site rules such as speeding limits, competent or unauthorised drivers
- ineffective audible or visual warning devices
- poorly marked or no indication of safe routes or walkways for pedestrians

Striking by moving, flying or falling objects - issues

- unsafe stacking of materials

- unsecured loads
- unsuitable or damaged pallets
- failure of storage materials racking
- ejected waste e.g. from milling, grinding or swarf
- moving or unstable components of machinery and plant
- incorrect methods of lifting or lowering materials
- work process affecting drivers and people e.g. dust being blown into eyes

Striking against fixed or stationary objects - issues

- presence of sharp edges of machinery, materials or plant
- storage issues for plant, tools and materials creating access and egress issues
- poor general and local lighting
- confined and restricted working room
- contact with crane pendants at head or body height

Conditions and environment hazards - issues

- poor workplace housekeeping and standards of hygiene
- environmental issues both internal and external
- vehicular movement alongside people and offices
- high risk activities such as construction, demolition, excavation and maintenance
- loading and unloading operations e.g. reversing lorries
- hazards associated with distribution centres, warehousing, depots, bus and freight terminals
- issues relating to open staircases and emergency access and egress routes

Control measures - movement of people

Movement of people - surfaces

Generic controls can be introduced for the safe movement of people in the workplace to avoid accidents such as the installation of slip resistant floors.

Anti-slip floors will only be effective if a high standard of maintenance is achieved. This can be carried out by providing slip resistant surfaces in the following areas:

- mats at entry points to absorb water brought in on footwear
- specific activities being carried out in the workplace
- designated walkways
- changes in levels, steps, vehicle access and ladders
- inclines such as ramps and slopes
- pedestrian and vehicle intersections
- maintenance access areas

Designated walkways - controls

Designated walkways need to be established and maintained to ensure a reasonably safe place to work. All designated walkways should be monitored to ensure that they are:

- free from obstructions
- clearly defined routes and marked with signage
- maintained to a high standard
- safe when being used
- consideration to other pedestrians
- vehicular movements at interchanges

Barriers - controls

Fencing and guarding should be erected where possible to effectively separate and segregate people from moving plant and machinery that may be affected by being exposed to:

- falls
- falling objects
- struck by moving objects such as vehicles, grab or robotic arms and moving parts of machinery

Signs and warning - controls

The use of signs and personal protective equipment must conform to any of the relevant regulatory requirements in order to ensure worker safety. They would include signs to indicate the precise hazards that workers are exposed to, and the personal protective equipment required such as:

- excavations
- change in levels and height
- demarcation of hazardous areas
- prohibited areas
- edges of steps
- overhead power lines and obstructions
- slip and trips hazards
- falling objects
- PPE - e.g. hard hats, footwear, eye protection, high visibility clothing and hearing protection

Access and egress - controls

All places of work should have an initial assessment of the hazards to ensure the safety of workers who are exposed to any specific or inherent hazards associated with the tasks or activities undertaken. In order to achieve a high standard of safety considerations need to be established to ensure:

- sufficient space to work and manoeuvre
- removal of slip and trip hazards such as cables or pipe work
- edge protection to prevent falls
- emergency procedures for work in confined spaces
- environmental considerations (e.g. heating, lighting, noise and dusts) has been carried out for all activities on site
- adequate storage for hand tools and equipment
- clearly signed and identifiable storage areas
- designated areas to be kept clear and marked such as emergency routes
- transparent or translucent panels and doors to prevent contact injuries
- safe means of escape e.g. from freezer rooms, confined spaces

Maintenance activities - controls

Large items of equipment may be required to have maintained specific parts and. therefore, the associated activities may require additional safety issues e.g. emergencies or evacuation. Considerations to such activities could include:

- effective pre-planning phase
- temporary signage displayed
- barriers and preventative measures into danger areas
- public protection where required
- environmental hazards assessed such as noise, heat, light, dusts, fumes or ultra violet light from welding
- competent supervision and monitoring and controlling the movement of people
- responding to the changing environment as the work progresses
- ensuring a high level of housekeeping is maintained

Section 5: Working at height

In this section:

1. Work activities involving working at height
2. Hazards and risks of working at height
3. Generic control measures
4. Ladders
5. Fixed scaffolding
6. Mobile tower - access platform
7. Mobile elevated work platform
8. Trestles
9. Staging platforms
10. Leading edge protection

Learning Outcomes

Explain the hazards and control measures for safe working at height

Work activities involving working at height

Typical workplace activities that involve working at height are:

- scaffold erecting and dismantling
- bricklaying
- painting and decorating
- steel erecting and installation
- demolition of structures
- roof work / fragile roofs / roof lights
- replacing or fitting of facia cladding

Hazards and risks of working at height

Risk depends on a number of factors such as:

- distance of fall
- weather conditions
- roof surface
- number of people working
- competence of people
- supervision of operation
- duration of work
- access and egress
- safe use of equipment e.g. ladders

Generic control measures

Considerations to ensure worker safety would include the provision of suitable and sufficient measures to prevent a fall such as:

- undertake a risk assessment and evaluate the likelihood and severity of a fall from any vertical distance
- minimise the distance and the consequences of the fall if it is probable that an injury could occur
- supervision and monitoring of the activities, but level of supervision / monitoring will depend upon the potential vertical distance
- methods of prevention of a fall such as Harness, lanyards, shock absorbers, edge protection, catch nets and bags will greatly reduce the injury sustained
- avoiding working in adverse weather conditions especially in high winds
- requirements for an emergency rescue
- precautions necessary to prevent falls and falling materials
- requirements for PPE e.g. head protection

Ladders

Ladders are only to be worked from if it is a Low Risk activity and not when two hands are required to undertake a task. They should not be used when:

- the work is at an excessive height
- the ladder cannot be secured or made stable
- the work is of a long duration
- the equipment or materials to be used are heavy or bulky
- the weather conditions are adverse
- there is no protection around moving vehicles

Selection of ladders

- suitable for surface conditions, task and environment.
- Class 1 for industrial work, EN131 for light work
- well maintained, no visible defects
- maintenance general inspection – records and ladder tagged
- use manufacturer's recommended stability devices
- ensure ladder is long enough; do not work off top 3 rungs or steps and ladder must extend 1 M above the 'work' area

Securing of ladders

- tie both stiles to a suitable point
- use of ladder stability device
- securely wedge the ladder
- secure at base e.g. foot the ladder or tied to a rigid support
- angle of ladder – 4 to 1 ratio (4 up to 1 away from the wall/structure)

Use of ladders

- aluminium ladders are light but should not be used in high winds or near live electricity
- timber ladders need regular inspection for damage and should not be painted
- ensure that the use of a ladder is the safest means of access for the work to be done and the height to be climbed
- ladder needs to be stable with a safe inclination (1 in 4)
- at least 1 m of ladder above the stepping off point
- over-reaching must be eliminated
- workers who are to use ladders must be trained in the correct method of use and selection
- ladders should be inspected (particularly for damaged or missing rungs) and maintained on a regular basis
- only to be repaired by competent persons
- ensure appropriate footwear e.g. good grip

Fixed scaffolding

Fixed scaffolds are usually independently tied. Important considerations are:

- scaffolding must only be erected and dismantled by competent people - any changes to the scaffold must also be done by a competent person
- erected on stable level ground
- adequate toe boards, guard rails and intermediate rails must be fitted to prevent people or materials from falling.
- the scaffold must rest on a stable surface; uprights should have base plates and timber sole plates if necessary
- there must be safe access and egress
- work platforms should be fully boarded with no tipping or tripping hazards

- scaffold should be sited away from or protected from traffic routes so that it is not damaged by vehicles
- the scaffold should be properly braced and secured to the building or structure
- not overloaded - within Safe Working Load (SWL)
- public must be protected at all stages of the work

Inspection

Only required if more that 2M high

Inspection of the scaffold must be made and recorded - 'scaftag' and written records in site office - and must be carried out when:

- first erected
- after significant alteration
- after event that may affect stability e.g. after high winds
- WEEKLY - 7 days

Fixed scaffolding - components

- standard
- ledger
- guard rail
- toe boards
- transom
- base plate
- sole board - ties
- working platform
- bracing

Mobile tower - access platform

Mobile tower scaffolding is independent scaffolding that is pre-fabricated and easily assembled. Considerations for use include:

- towers must be tied to a rigid structure if exposed to windy weather
- persons working from a tower must not over-reach or use ladders from the work platform
- safe distances must be maintained between the tower and overhead power lines both during working operations and when the tower is moved
- tower should be inspected on a regular basis with appropriate report
- not to be overloaded, refer to Safe Working Load (SWL)
- wheels locked
- don't move when in use
- erected by competent person
- cordon off area when there is a chance of people entering the working area
- don't use close to vehicle movements
- don't block emergency exits or access/egress routes

Mobile elevated work platform

The following factors must be considered when using mobile elevated work platforms:

- only be operated by trained and competent persons
- never be moved in the elevated position
- operated on level and stable ground
- tyres must be properly inflated and the wheels immobilized
- outriggers should be fully extended and locked in position

- due care must be exercised with overhead power supplies and obstructions
- procedures should be in place in the event of machine failure e.g. emergency rescue
- cordon off area
- don't use close to vehicle movements
- don't block emergency exits or access/egress routes

Trestles

Made from pre-fabricated steel, wood or aluminium.

Control measures for working from trestles would include the following considerations:

- equipment checked for damage before use
- set up on firm and level ground
- consider floor surface before erecting e.g. is the floor slippery?
- provision of boards on soft ground
- ensure that the trestle has been erected in accordance with instructions and training methods
- all locking pins are in place Under no circumstances:
- apply side forces such as pushing or pulling, there is a risk of toppling over
- exceed the safe working load of the platform, which includes the person and tools or materials

Staging platforms

In all scenarios the following considerations and observations should be made to ensure safety:

- sufficient size and working room and use of equipment or materials

- prevention of gaps where a person or materials could fall through
- fitted with toe boards and handrails
- free from slip and trip hazards
- good housekeeping
- ensure that load is not exceeded and that waste materials are removed from the staging
- erected on firm level ground to maintain stability
- use of boards to spread any load where soft ground has been identified

Leading edge protection

Whilst working close to edges that are not protected create significant risks. Therefore appropriate controls must be put into place:

- any work of this nature should be avoided where possible;
- otherwise careful planning and the development of a safe system of work provided so that suitable arrangements are in place to carry out the work safely
- individuals can be prevented from falling by harness and lanyard

Catch nets

Catch nets are one of the preferred options for working at the leading edge. They provide protection for all workers in the vicinity or roof. Any netted system provided should be erected by a competent person where evaluations of the potential combined weight of persons and materials falling and should be strong enough to take the weight calculated.

- any system should include the use of harnesses attached to a suitable fixing point and effective supervision in high risk areas throughout the work activity.

Section 6: Excavations

In this section:

1. Hazards and risks of excavations
2. Controls

Learning Outcomes

Explain the hazards of, and control measures for, excavations

Hazards and risks of excavations

Working in or around excavations, trenches, basements, underground silos, tanks, vats, manholes and sewers will pose several issues:

- people falling from height into the excavation due to inadequate or no edge protection
- materials and soil stored too close to the excavation increasing stress on the excavation sides
- undermining foundations of adjacent buildings and structures
- plant and machinery falling into the excavation due to collapsing sides - vehicle bump stops not established
- collapse of sides
- contact with underground services – e.g. water, gas, electricity
- lack of supervision and no clear signage
- access or egress
- flooding – from extreme weather
- contaminated land, water and chemicals
- biological hazards – e.g. leptospirosis (Weil's Disease)
- lack of oxygen and build-up of fumes e.g. from vehicle exhausts

Controls - excavations

The provision of safe systems of work to control the associated hazards in order to achieve a good standard of safety would include:

- buried services - service location drawings made available and electronic detection equipment e.g. CAT Scanner
- Permit-to-Work (dig) and hand over procedures in place
- exclusion zones to ensure persons not involved with the activity are kept out
- provision of a suitable support for the excavation e.g. shoring, trench boxes, benching
- inspection reports and checks made at the beginning of each working day and recorded,
- control vehicular movement around the excavation, provision of edge protection to prevent falls
- emergency planning arrangements
- competence of staff and supervision
- safe digging practices would normally be required to ensure worker safety
- barriers, temporary lighting, clearly marked signs, vehicle 'stops'
- spoil removed has been placed at a safe location clear of the excavation, sloping the sides
- re-positioning plant and equipment away from excavation
- provision of personal protective equipment e.g. gloves
- use of pumps in case of flooding
- consideration of contaminated land e.g. buried asbestos
- biological hazard control - pest (rat) control
- testing of oxygen levels or gases e.g. vehicle exhausts
- safe crossing points across the excavation for pedestrians and vehicles
- safe access and egress

Chapter 7 - Transport Hazards and Risk Controls

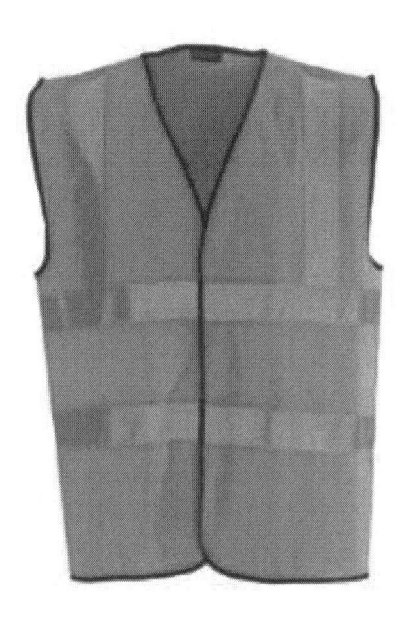

Section 1: Safe movement of vehicles

In this section:

1. Hazards from transport operations
2. Common failings / control measures

Learning Outcomes

Explain the hazards and control measures for the safe movement of people in the workplace

Hazards from transport operations

There are several kinds of ways in which workers can be seriously injured or killed in the workplace by transport related accidents some of which include:

- pedestrians and fixed objects being struck by the moving vehicle
- falling from the vehicle
- vehicle collapse or overturn
- falling materials from the vehicle
- being struck by the vehicle whilst driving it or as a passenger

Influencing factors

Typical factors that can cause accidents with vehicular movement are:

- insecure or unstable loads
- travelling with an elevated load - e.g. on Fork Lift Truck
- loading and unloading operations
- colliding with other vehicles

- human error and loss of control
- kerbs and structures e.g. lamp post, signs etc.
- obstructions
- cornering at speed
- braking hard
- inclines, declines and uneven surfaces
- ground conditions e.g. uneven, wet, icy etc.
- mechanical failure or malfunction
- sheeting (high sided vehicles) and coupling of trailers
- vehicle maintenance work

Common failings / control measures

The main reasons for transport operational control failure are:

- lack of speed bumps / restrictors
- vision - mirrors on vehicles and wall mounted crossing places and safe walkways clearly marked and separated where possible
- protective barriers to prevent pedestrians from walking into the paths of moving vehicles at egress doors
- safe method of loading such as drive through systems where possible to limit reversing
- banksman to supervise reversing vehicles
- only authorised and competent persons are in the vehicle manoeuvring area
- maintain road surfaces by removing compacted dirt, oils, products and debris, any pot holes have been identified and filled in with suitable material
- maintenance of vehicles pre-user checks have been completed and recorded by the user
- poor selection of vehicle and protection devices such as seat restraints, roll over protection

- protected warehousing storage racking standards - collapse due to collisions from vehicles
- competency levels persons driving and pedestrians

Safe Site - issues

- plan your workplace so that pedestrians are safe from vehicles
- provide a one-way system
- provide separate routes for pedestrians and vehicles where possible
- provide reversing area
- provide appropriate crossing
- use 'Highway Code' signs to indicate vehicle routes, speed limits, pedestrian crossings, etc.
- make sure lighting is adequate where people and vehicles are working
- make sure road surfaces are firm and even
- make sure there are safe areas for loading and unloading
- try to provide separate car parking for visitors as they may not know your site

Safe Driver - issues

- train operators and ensure competence
- reassess lift truck operators at regular intervals, e.g. every three to five years, or when new risks arise such as changes to working practices
- train drivers of other vehicles to a similar standard
- make sure all drivers are supervised (including those visiting the site)

Safe vehicle - issues

- ensure vehicles are suitable for the purpose for which they are used

- maintain vehicles in good repair, particularly the braking system, steering, tyres, lights, mirrors and specific safety systems
- remove the need for people to climb up on vehicles where possible, e.g. by providing gauges and controls that are accessible from ground level
- reduce the risk of falling when people have to climb onto a vehicle or trailer by providing well-constructed ladders, non-slip walkways and guard rails where possible
- provide reversing aids such as CCTV where appropriate
- fit rollover protective structures and use seat belts where fitted

Section 2: Driving at work

In this section:

1. Common driving hazards
2. Control of driving

Learning Outcomes

Outline the factors associated with driving at work that increase the risk of an incident and the; control measures to reduce work driving risks

Common Driving Hazards

- driving on different sides of the roads - e.g. in Europe
- consideration of international signs or signals in different languages
- weather conditions
- welfare arrangements whilst travelling
- working excessive hours
- travelling through the day or night

- valuable cargo
- driver fatigue
- stress due to traffic, tight timescales etc.

Control Measures - driving

- policy that covers work-related road safety; policies for severe weather conditions
- risk assessment to evaluating the risks to the driver
- driver competency, fitness and health, training
- suitability of the vehicle, its condition, safety equipment
- driver checks of vehicles
- safety critical information, or ergonomic considerations
- the journey routes and the distance
- weather conditions
- driving hours, work schedules and number of breaks
- policies for severe weather conditions
- control measures to reduce work-related driving risks
- monitoring driver performance to ensure collection of vital driving information
- reporting of work-related road incidents by employees
- employers responsibilities for work-related road safety
- legal responsibilities of individuals whilst on public roads

Chapter 8 - Musculoskeletal Hazards and Risk Control

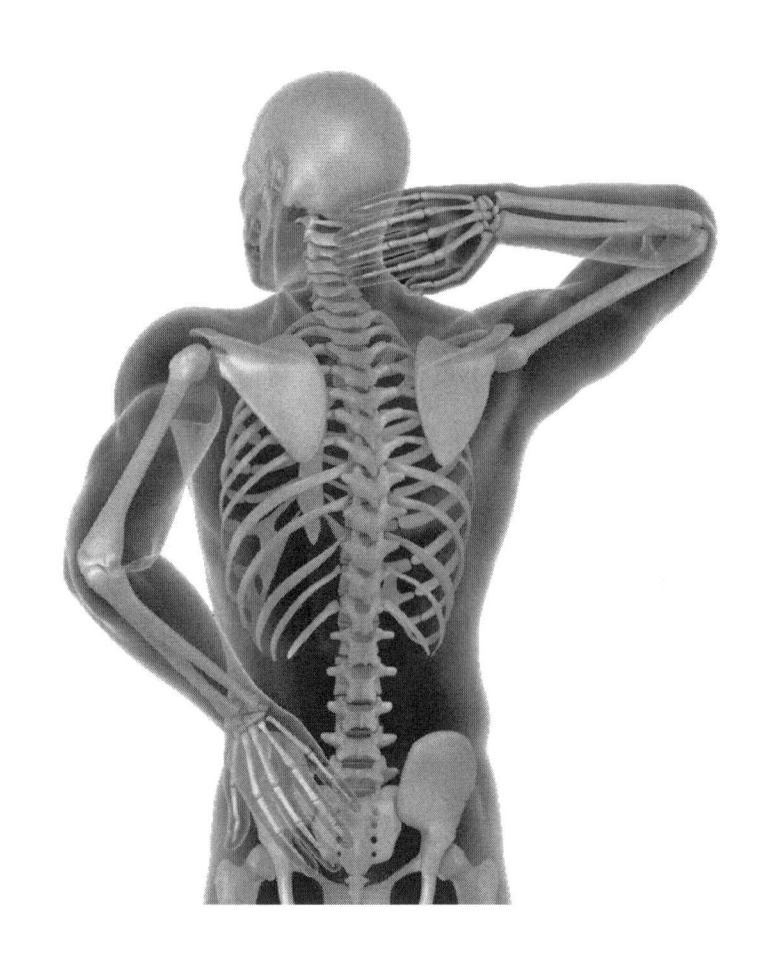

Section 1: Work related upper limb disorders

In this section:

1. Risk factors
2. Types of injury
3. Display Screen Equipment (DSE)
4. DSE Risk Assessment

Learning Outcomes

Explain the processes and practices that may lead to work-related upper limb disorders and the appropriate control measures

Risk factors

The term Work Related Upper Limb Disorder (WRULD) is often used as being synonymous with a large number of conditions including; Repetitive Strain Injury (RSI) and Cumulative Trauma Disorder.

The risk factors for all of the above conditions are more-or-less the same:

- **static muscle loading** i.e. excessive loading of the muscles
- **poor posture** e.g. badly designed work stations
- **awkward movements** e.g. poorly designed tools
- **overuse and repetition** i.e. continual and prolonged usage of one set of muscles and tendons
- **stress** i.e. people who are under stress increase muscle tension hence exacerbate the problem

Situations that are likely to show signs of WRULD are:
- excessive and prolonged operations e.g. using keyboard, excessive use of hand tools
- assembly of small components
- construction activities involving prolonged and heavy lifting e.g. bricklaying

Generic controls to prevent WRULD

Generic controls will include a combination of:

- job rotation
- taking regular breaks
- health monitoring
- keeping warm
- exercising of the muscles and tendons e.g. warm ups!
- reducing the load bearing
- reduce excessive over-reaching and stretching
- redesign of the task

Types of injury

Tenosynovitis

- inflammation of the fluid filled sheath (called the synovial sheath) that surrounds a tendon
- symptoms of tenosynovitis include pain, swelling and difficulty moving the particular joint where the inflammation occurs. When the condition causes the finger to 'stick' in a fixed position, this is commonly known as 'trigger finder'.

Carpal tunnel syndrome (CTS)

- when the median nerve is trapped or compressed in the carpel tunnel by the inflammation of tendons

- main symptom are intermittent numbness and tingling of the thumb, index, long and radial half of the ring finger

de Quervain's syndrome

- a 'type' of tenosynovitis
- inflammation of tendons in the thumb that extend to the wrist
- swollen tendons and their coverings rub against the narrow tunnel through which they pass
- result is pain at the base of the thumb and extending into the lower arm

Thoracic outlet syndrome

- group of disorders that occur when the blood vessels or nerves in the thoracic outlet, the space between the collarbone and first rib, become compressed.
- can cause pain in the shoulders and neck and numbness in the fingers

Display Screen Equipment (DSE)

When setting up a workstation, the following will need to be considered:

- Lighting
- Contrast
- Noise
- Legroom
- Window
- Screen
- Software
- Keyboard
- Work surface
- Work chair
- Foot rest

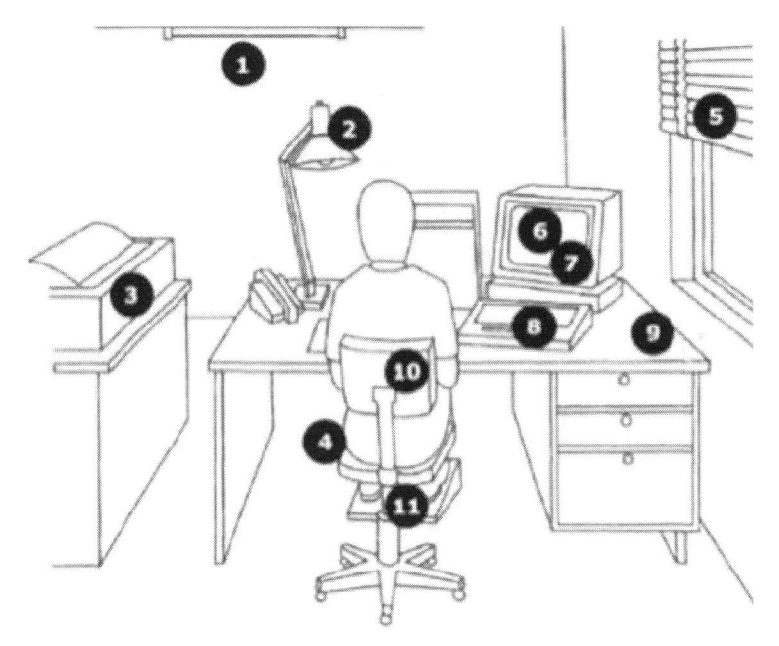

Source: HSE

Employers' responsibilities

- analyse workstations to assess and reduce risks
- make sure controls are in place;
- provide information and training to users
- provide eyesight and eye tests on request, and special spectacles if needed
- review the assessment when the user or DSE changes

Issues of using DSE equipment

- ergonomic - static in one position for long periods of time - issues especially with pregnant women
- WRULD
- eye strain - continually looking at the screen and glare
- stress
- environmental issues e.g. noise

- epilepsy - cannot cause but can exacerbate the issue

DSE Risk assessment

When undertaking a DSE Workstation Assessment the following points will need to be considered:

Screen

- comfortable to read
- stable image
- adjustable image
- adjustable position
- free from glare and reflections

Key board

- separate from screen
- comfortable keying position
- user technique
- legibility of key characters

Mouse / tracker ball

- suitable for use
- positioned near user
- works smoothly
- adjustable response
- room to rest wrist

Software

- suitable for the task
- responsive and user friendly

Furniture

- adequate space
- properly organised
- glare free surfaces
- stable fully adjustable chair

User position

- eyes level with top of screen
- forearms horizontal over desk surface
- feet flat on floor / foot rest
- mouse / trackball
- suitable for use
- positioned near user
- works smoothly
- adjustable response
- room to rest wrist

Section 2: Manual handling

In this section:

1. Common types of injury
2. Assessment of manual handling activities
3. Effective lifting technique

Learning Outcomes

Explain the hazards and control measures which should be considered when assessing risks from manual handling

Common types of injury

Types of over-three-day injury caused by manual handling accidents 2001/02

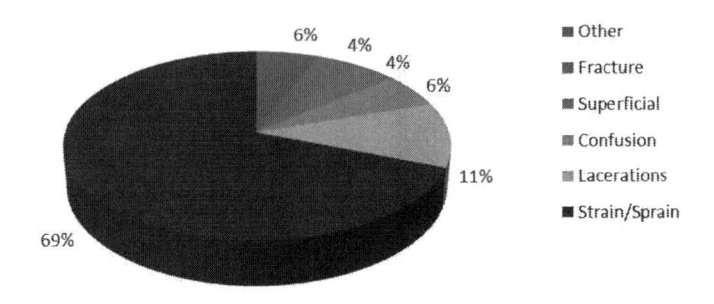

- 69% Strain/Sprain
- 11% Lacerations
- 6% Confusion
- 4% Superficial
- 4% Fracture
- 6% Other

Kinds of Accidents over a 3 day period

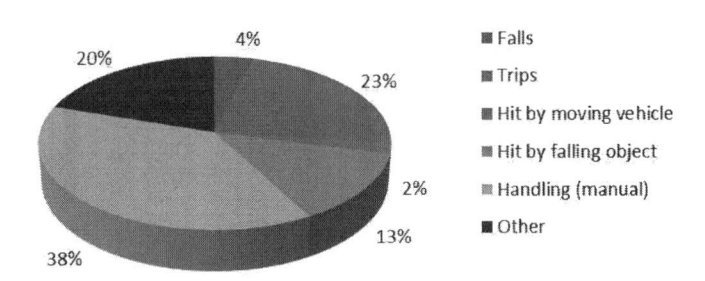

- 23% Falls
- 2% Trips
- 13% Hit by moving vehicle
- 38% Hit by falling object
- 20% Handling (manual)
- 4% Other

Source: HSE

The actual injuries caused by incorrect manual handling are:

- hernia
- ruptures
- torn ligaments, tendon strain or sprain
- spinal compression / prolapsed disc (sometimes called a slipped disc)
- muscle strain

- crushing, cuts or abrasions (from dropping or sharp edges of load)

Manual handling assessment

Consideration should be given to the following FOUR factors; often referred to as TILE:

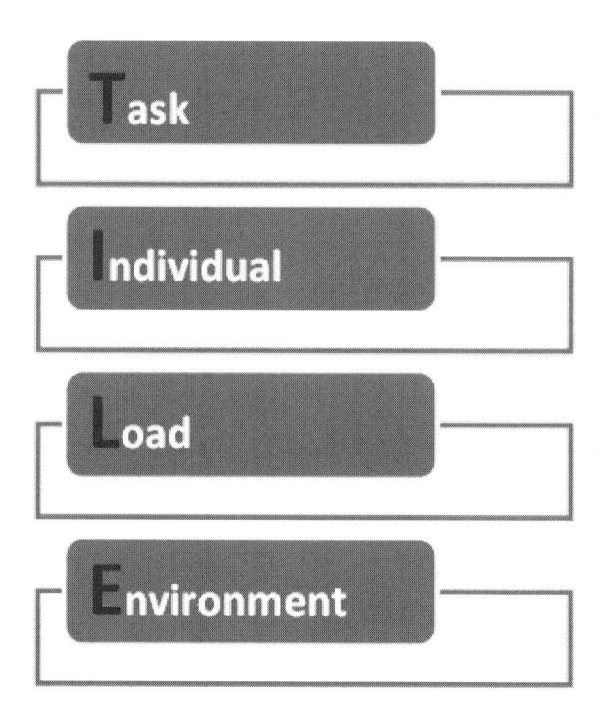

- **Task**
- **Individual**
- **Load**
- **Environment**

Task - considerations

- repetition of task
- rest/recovery time
- effort to start or stop load moving
- negotiating slopes, corners etc.
- does the task require unusual capability

Individual - considerations

- competence of workers
- vulnerable groups such as: young persons, disabled, old persons
- individual capabilities e.g. fitness
- pre-existing illness such as bad back or health issues
- new or expectant mothers

Load - considerations

- size or shape
- weight of the load
- what is the load - live load (animal), fluid, stability
- are there sharp edges, hot, cold
- difficult to hold - use of handles?
- is the load secure and stable and where is the centre of gravity

Environment - considerations

- very hot or cold environments
- changes in levels whilst carrying
- negotiating steps and steep slopes
- rough surfaces
- moving vehicles
- sudden gusts of wind
- adequate lighting or excessive noise

Effective lifting technique

- think before handling / lifting
- assess the load e.g. weight, how to grip etc.
- plan the lift/handling activity
- keep the load close to the waist
- adopt a stable position

- ensure a good hold on the load
- moderate flexion of back, hips and knees at start of lift
- don't flex the back any further while lifting
- avoid twisting the back or leaning sideways especially while the back is bent
- keep the head up when handling
- move smoothly
- don't handle more than can be easily managed
- put down and then, if necessary, adjust the load

Section 3: Mechanically operated lifting and moving equipment

In this section:

1. Hazards and risks of common types of loading equipment

Learning Outcomes

Explain the hazards, precautions and control measures to reduce the risk in the use of lifting and moving equipment with specific reference to manually operated load and moving

Hazards and risks of common types of loading equipment

Hazards

- Pulling and pushing - causing sprains and strains
- Falling loads - causing crush injuries through contact

Control measures

- careful selection of such equipment

- person using this type of equipment appropriately trained and competent.

Inspections

Inspections should be carried out by a competent person to determine whether the equipment can be; operated, adjusted and maintained safely. This should be done annually by a competent person.

Pallet truck

Pallet Trucks are another very simple method of lifting and moving loads around the workplace with ease. Typical pallet trucks are hydraulic manual pump action or battery operated

Section 4: Lifting and moving equipment

In this section:

1. Lifting equipment - general considerations
2. Statutory testing
3. Fork Lift Trucks (FLTs)
4. Lifts and hoists
5. Conveyors
6. Steel rollers
7. Cranes

Learning Outcomes

Explain the hazards, precautions and control measures to reduce the risk in the use of lifting and moving equipment with specific reference to mechanically operated load and moving equipment.

General considerations

Lifting equipment is best described as equipment that is used to lift or lower a load. Types of lifting equipment include, but not restricted to;

- cranes, FLTs, lifting block and tackle, overhead gantry crane, materials or goods hoist, people handling cradles, hoists and lift shafts
- loads must be secured and balanced
- equipment (including lifting hooks and slings) should be visually checked by a competent person wear-and-tear and damage
- shackles and eyebolts correctly tightened
- operators must be competent
- regular inspections of tackle should be made in addition to the mandatory thorough examinations - covered in later section
- when not in use, equipment (including slings, ropes etc.) must be stored correctly
- equipment should be tested, formally inspected and visually checked prior to use.
- a report or record (certificate) should be made of the formal inspections, which should be kept (at least) until the next inspection.
- unless stated otherwise, lifts and hoists should be visually inspected every week - see Statutory Test
- all parts of the equipment must be strong, stable and capable of lifting the load
- suitable equipment for the task
- positioned and installed correctly e.g. on firm level ground
- appropriately marked, e.g. with safe working load
- ensure lifting operations are planned, supervised and carried out in safe manner

- competent staff to undertake and supervise the lifting operation

Inspections

- carried out by a competent person to determine whether the equipment can be operated, adjusted and maintained safely
- carried out when erected
- at least annually
- lifting accessories every 6 months
- certificate required
- report or record should be kept at least until the next inspection

Statutory inspection and testing

Lifting Operations and Lifting Equipment Regulations (LOLER) 1998.

Very wide definition of Lifting Equipment and includes; anything from a crane to a rope and all associated attachments.

Lifting equipment - means work equipment for lifting or lowering loads and includes attachments used for anchoring, fixing or supporting it. Very wide definition - from a crane to a rope and all associated attachments.

Regulations require:

- thorough examination with report, and if appropriate written scheme of lifting equipment: the detailed and specialised examination by a competent person
- before it is put into service for the first time
- after installation or reassembly

- during its exposure to conditions which cause deterioration
- evidence of the last examination when the equipment is used outside the undertaking
- re-examination - for lifting persons every 6 months; other lifting equipment every 12 months

Fork Lift Trucks (FLTs)

The hazards associated with fork trucks include:

- driving too fast and cornering speeds
- sudden and sharp breaking
- driving down steep slopes forwards or across slopes
- driving with an elevated load
- collisions with structures e.g. racking, other vehicles and pedestrians
- overloading and insecure loads, nature of load e.g. liquid
- poorly maintained vehicles
- road / ground surfaces
- mechanical failures due to a lack of maintenance
- driving over ramps and kerbs
- 'street furniture' e.g. lamp posts
- hazards associated with the truck itself e.g. batteries (acid and electricity), diesel fumes, propane gas
- overhead obstructions

Protection of pedestrians

In order to ensure that all workers, pedestrians or others are safe suitable control measures need to be strictly adhered to due to the hazards associated with fork trucks. Consideration as to those arrangements include:

- responsible person to be in control of the fork truck operating area

- selection and suitable vehicle for task
- operating areas to be wide enough, unobstructed, vision panels, translucent doors at access points, wall-mounted mirrors
- key control policy and not leaving keys in the ignition when unattended
- daily recorded pre-use checks by operator
- separate routes, one-way systems, crossing points, traffic lights, barriers and clearly marked
- competent drivers, approved course
- fork truck operating areas to be maintained and adequately illuminated
- adequate signs and markings in vehicle manoeuvring areas, crossing points and directions of travel
- designated parking areas for all fork trucks when not in use
- high visibility jackets for pedestrians
- vehicle fitted with warning lights, mirrors, horns

Electric FLTs

Specific issues include:

- battery acid - corrosive, use of PPE e.g. goggles, gloves
- generation of hydrogen gas giving risk to an explosion hazard - area must be well ventilated
- short circuiting of batteries - must be insulated e.g. plastic caps, connectors well maintained
- manual handling of batteries

Diesel FLTs

Specific issues include:

- fumes and particulates - area must be well ventilated
- dermatitis from the diesel

Propane FLTs

Specific issues include:

- flammability of the propane in gas cylinder; also consider storage of gas bottles
- manual handling of the cylinders

Lifts and hoists

A lift (or hoist) has a platform or cage controlled by guides and may carry passengers and/or be stand-alone. They must have:

- interlocking doors (i.e. wired in to the control system)
- doors/gates must be closed before movement
- if carrying passengers, fitted with an automatic braking system to prevent overrunning
- in the event of suspension / rope failure to be fitted with a safety device to support the structure
- be maintained by competent persons with written records (certification)
- must protect 'others' during maintenance operations e.g. from falling down the lift shaft
- all the items for lifting are maintained by a competent person. e.g. chain slings, rope slings, eyebolts, shackles, wires and ropes

Conveyors

The main hazards with conveyors are:

- clothing or limbs being drawn into the mechanical or moving parts of the machinery or equipment
- coming into contact with rollers causing cuts and abrasions

- being struck by falling objects if the conveyor is overhead
- manual handling issues in loading and unloading activities
- exposure to high-frequency noise levels
- maintained through a scheme or series of recorded checks
- all rotating or dangerous parts are guarded
- connected to a system of emergency stops, along the entire length of the conveyor, so that the conveyor can be stopped immediately if required or in the event of an emergency
- regular daily checks carried out as to the condition of the belt conveyor

Steel rollers

The controls include:

- that all nip guards are in place
- damaged or worn bearings have been replaced
- operated by a competent person
- maintained through a scheme or series of recorded checks
- free running roller conveyor has pop out rollers at nip points for safety

Cranes

The key points are: operator inspection prior to each use – crane and lifting tackle

- when not in use - do not leave loads suspended
- area around 'lift' to be free from people and obstacles
- never carry loads over people
- maintained at regular intervals and results recorded
- ensure Statutory test certificate and inspection of crane and tackle (LOLER)

- good visibility and communications. Possible use of *'banksman'*
- only lift loads vertically
- travel with load close to the ground
- switch off power to crane when unattended
- competency of operators
- Safe Working Load (SWL) not exceeded
- see also Lifting Tackle – below as part of the crane

Crane failure

The main causes of crane failure are:

- overloading / Safe Working Load exceeded
- poor slinging of load / unbalanced
- unstable ground
- collision with another structure
- contact with overhead power lines
- ground/foundation failure
- structural failure of the crane
- operator error
- lack of maintenance and/or regular inspections

Chapter 9 - Work Equipment Hazards and Risk Control

Section 1: General requirements of work equipment

In this section:

1. Scope of work equipment
2. Suitability of work equipment
3. Machine Control systems
4. Provision of information, instruction and training
5. Machine Maintenance
6. Examination and Testing
7. Pressure systems

Learning Outcomes

Outline the general requirement for work equipment

Scope of work equipment

Provision and Use of Work Equipment Regulations 1998 - often referred to as PUWER.

The definition of work equipment includes:
- hand-tools
- power tools
- machinery

Suitability of work equipment

Equipment must be suitable for the task. When assessing suitability the following will need consideration:

- fit and suitable for the task and reference to
- initial and on-going integrity; place where it will be used; purpose for which it will be used

- only used for specified / identified operations
- health and safety of the user must be considered e.g. ergonomic issues
- easily maintained
- pre-use inspection produced
- formal inspection at regular intervals
- competency of operators - information, instruction and training
- guarding against dangerous parts
- provision of controls to isolate power and emergency stop controls
- the stability of the equipment, i.e. will not 'fall down'
- the environment in which it is being used, e.g. well lit, housekeeping
- suitable warning markings or device e.g. flashing lights

Machine control systems

Machines need to be stopped and started on a routine basis and during emergencies and appropriate to machine and operation. Controls must be:

- in a safe position
- easy to identify and understand

Stop controls

- when isolated the machine will be in a safe condition
- the stop control will have priority over any operating or start control

Emergency stop controls

- must be at key control or operating points
- must be in appropriate location
- easily reached and actuated (activated)

- clearly visible

Provision of information, instruction and supervision

Specific training needs need to be developed and implemented for all machines that will include:

- identification of specific hazards and risks and will include machine and non-machine
- written instructions e.g. safe system of work; pre-use checks; start; stop; safe running
- easily accessible information
- comprehensible and easily understood, and if necessary in different languages
- supervisors / managers to assess competence and record
- manufacturer's manuals / instructions

Machine maintenance

All machines need to be adequately maintained. It is not possible to give a definite list for all machines but the following are the main considerations

- design machinery to reduce need to remove guards
- type, age (of the equipment) and usage
- planned preventative maintenance – how and what needs to be done at pre-determined intervals to maintain safety and integrity
- competence of people carrying out maintenance operations, adequate supervision
- equipment must be made safe before maintenance begins e.g. locking-off
- Permit To Work (PTW), suitable PPE may be required, isolation of pipes and power

- correct tools must be used for maintenance tasks, lifting handling equipment
- restrict access to non-maintenance staff – e.g. cordon off area
- refer to manufacturers' recommendations for maintenance schedules
- release stored energy (e.g. pressure), allow machine to cool down, purge and ventilate
- access issues e.g. is scaffolding required?
- operating environment (e.g. adequate lighting), maintain during quite periods or 'annual shut down'
- risks from malfunction or failure
- criticality of the equipment to the process

Examination and Testing

Machines must be tested on a regular basis to show they are fit-for-purpose. The manufacturer's guidelines will indicate how often testing should take place and what needs to be tested. The following will be the minimum requirements:

- stop controls working
- emergency stops working
- integrity of machine
- statutory test e.g. if it is lifting equipment
- what is expected of operators e.g. visual inspection and start up checks

Pressure Systems

Pressure Systems Safety Regulations 2000 (PSSR)

Examples - boilers, pressurised process plant, pressure cookers, valves, steam traps

- equipment suitable and safe

- periodic examination of boilers and air receivers supplied with correct written information (scheme) and markings
- know operating conditions and use within safe operating limits
- use of protective devices e.g. valves, gauges
- written scheme of maintenance
- certified / examined by a competent person and report / certificate

Section 2: Hand held tools

In this section:

1. Hazards and risks of hand held tools

Learning Outcomes

Explain the hazards and control of hand-held tools

Hazards and risks of hand-held tools

Hand-held tools are all tools used by hand e.g. chisels, hammers, mallets.

The following is a synopsis of the issues associated with such tools:

- right tool for the job and environment
- broken parts e.g. handles, heads
- cutting edges must be sharp e.g. knives, chisels
- must be 'clean' – especially free from oil and grease (e.g. on handles)
- maintenance
- cutting tools – regular sharpening
- adjustable tools – appropriate lubricating

- mushroomed (cold) chisel heads – regular grinding
- appropriate storage
- compatibility with other tools e.g. hammer and chisel
- pre-use checks e.g. sharpness of chisel, broken handle
- formal periodic inspection
- quarantine if tools are damaged

Section 3: Machinery hazards

In this section

1. Mechanical and non-mechanical hazards
2. Chain saw
3. Photocopier
4. Document shredder
5. Portable electric drill
6. Cement mixer
7. Portable electric sander
8. Bench top grinder
9. Bench mounted drill
10. Strimmer
11. Compacter / bailer

Learning Outcomes

Describe the main mechanical and non-mechanical hazards of machinery

Mechanical and non-mechanical hazards

There are two categories:

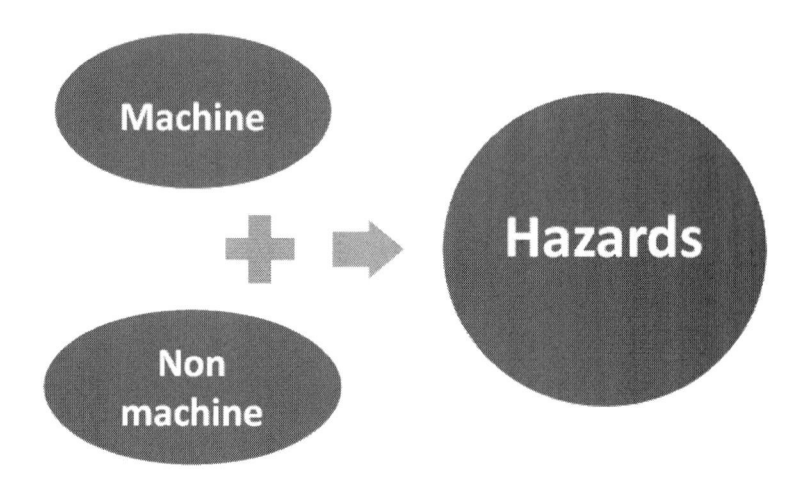

- Machine Hazards
- Non-machine Hazards

Machine hazards

- Rotating parts – giving rise to entanglement, friction burns,
- Ejection– giving rise to puncture or stabbing
- Sharp edges – giving rise to cuts or severing of fingers
- Moving parts – crushing, drawing-in

Non-machine hazards

- chemicals
- dust / mists / fumes
- electricity
- ergonomic issues e.g. awkward movements, access to all parts of machine, adequate working space
- high or low temperature
- manual handling e.g. gripping of machine, weight of machine – if being carried
- micro-organisms

- noise
- pressure
- radiation – ionising and non-ionising
- stored energy e.g. kinetic energy
- vibration

Chain saw

Machine Hazard	Non-machine Hazard
• cutting / severing • saw kicking back • entanglement • ejected wood chippings	• manual handling • noise • vibration • electricity • petrol hazards • hot engine and exhaust • environmental hazards – weather • falling branches – if cutting down trees

Photocopier

Machine Hazard	Non-machine Hazard
• entanglement • trapping in machine whilst cleaning	• electricity • hot surfaces • chemicals – from toner / ink

Document Shredder

Machine Hazard	Non-machine Hazard
• rotating parts • sharp edges • moving parts	• electricity • trailing cable • manual handling issues whilst emptying

Portable electric drill

Machine Hazard	Non-machine Hazard
• entanglement with rotating part e.g. rotating chuck • puncture – by drill bit • ejection – of material, broken drill or chuck key	• electricity • noise • vibration – hammer drill • dust • heat – drill bit and work piece • trailing cable – trip hazard • manual handling • drilling into hidden services e.g. electric cables • environmental hazards e.g. exposure to weather

Cement Mixer

Machine Hazard	Non-machine Hazard
• entanglement with rotating part • ejection of mixture	• electricity or petrol • noise • stability of mixer • cement dust - inhalation • cement - corrosive and irritant • trailing cable – trip hazard • manual handling and ergonomic issues • environmental hazards e.g. exposure to weather • uneven ground around mixer and moving vehicles

Portable electric sander

Machine Hazard	Non-machine Hazard
• abrasion • entanglement – rotating disc • drawing in – belt sander	• noise • vibration • electricity • trailing cable – trip hazard • manual handling / ergonomic • environmental hazards e.g. exposure to weather

Bench top grinder

Machine Hazard	Non-machine Hazard
• contact with rotating wheel • trap between wheel and rest • entanglement around axle • ejection of parts of work piece or from burst wheel	• dust • sparks / fire • electricity • noise • vibration • stability of machine • positioning / working posture

Bench Mounted Drill

Machine Hazard	Non-machine Hazard
• puncture from drill bit • entanglement • traps in belt drive • ejection - work piece, broken drill bit, or chuck key • cutting - work piece edges or swarf • impact / crushing from work table	• manual handling of work piece • heat generated by drilling • electricity • noise • vibration • dust (if drilling timber) • cutting fluid (often mineral oil) effects can be irritant • stability of pedestal drill

(Bench Mounted Drill - sometimes called bench drill / pedestal drill)

Strimmer

Machine Hazard	Non-machine Hazard
• impact / cutting from cutting line • trapping in motor and drive shaft • entanglement • ejection - stones / debris	• manual handling • noise • vibration • electricity or petrol • biological hazards e.g. dog poo!

Compactor/bailer

Machine Hazard	Non-machine Hazard
• crushing • entrapment • cutting - (shear) between ram and cas sides	• manual handling during loading and unloading • electrical • biological hazards from contaminated waste • noise • pressure - failure of hydraulic hoses

Section 4: Control measures for reducing risks

In this section:

1. Basic principles of machine guarding
2. Types of guards
3. Other machine protection devices

Learning Outcomes

Explain the main control measures for reducing the risks from machinery hazards

Basic principles of machine guarding

The basic principles of machine guarding are:

- must suitable for their purpose and of sound construction
- good construction, sound material and adequate strength
- maintained in an efficient state, in efficient working order and in good repair
- does not increased risk
- not easily bypassed or disabled
- sufficient distance from the danger zone
- not restrict the view of the machines operating cycle
- allow safe access for maintenance work
- easy to maintain

Types of Guard

Fixed guard

Key Features	Examples
• physical barrier around moving parts • not connected to the control system of the machine • physically attached to the machine • requires a specialist tool to remove **Merits** - completely encloses the danger area, requires specialist tool to remove **Disadvantages** – easy to remove if not in place machine will operate, easy to remove is tool available	• around a drive belt

Self-closing guard

Key Features	Examples
• closes as machine starts • guard sometimes 'sweeps' person away from danger zone	• around a circular saw

Adjustable guard

Key Features	Examples
• adjusted by the operator as required	• around a moving part of a machine

Interlocking guard

Key Features	Examples
• wired into the machines control system • machine cannot operate until in place • opening the guard - machine stops - or guard cannot be opened until the machine stopped • closing of the guard does not by itself restart the machine **Merits** - cannot operate machine until guard is in place, allows for regular and easy access **Disadvantages** - can be over-ridden by operator, machine may not stop when guard opened, requires regular maintenance and setting, if large guard then person can enter danger area and another person can start the machine	• microwave door • photo-copier door • see below – when guard opened lathe stop

Other machine protection devices

Trip device

Key Features	Examples
• when person enters area machine stops • operates when person enters 'danger' zone • wired into the electrical system of the machine • must be re-set after activated **Merits** - minimise the severity of the injury, can be used as an additional safety device **Disadvantages** - can be over-ridden, does not prevent harm as machine may not stop immediately, stops production hence causes delays to process, if tripping out regularly then increased stress of operator	• light curtain • pressure matt

Two handed control

Key Features	Examples
• requires operator to use both hands to operate controls • wired into the electrical system of the machine	• lawn mowers two hand to control

Push sticks

Key Features	Examples
• operator to push item into machine therefore keeping a safe distance from the machine	• push-stick

Chapter 10 - Electrical safety

Section 1: Principles of electricity

In this section:

1. Principles of electricity
2. Effects of electricity
3. Treatment of electric shock
4. Electrical safety devices
5. Main causes of electric fires in the workplace

Learning Outcomes

Outline the principles, hazards and risks associated when working with electrical systems or using electrical equipment

Principles of electricity

- current (symbol I) is measured in amps (symbol A or I) and is the amount of electricity
- resistance (symbol R) is measured in ohms (symbol Ω).
- resistance is the degree by which the electricity is prevented from flowing
- potential (symbol V) is measured in volts (symbol V).
- the potential is the degree of 'push' of electricity through a conductor or insulator
- power (symbol P) - measured in watts (symbol W)
- conductors - electricity will flow easily, e.g. copper wire, metals
- insulators - very poor conductors e.g. wood
- short circuit - is an electrical circuit that allows a current to travel along an unintended path
- mains voltage (UK) – 230V (220/240)
- **DC** – Direct Current i.e. the current goes in one direction e.g. from battery

- **AC** – Alternating Current i.e. current goes one way then the other; 50 times a second (Hertz); e.g. mains electricity

Ohm's law

Ohm's law can be summarised as the relationships between, V, I & R; and represented by:

- $V = I \times R$

Effects of electricity

- torn muscles, ligaments or cartilage
- interference with heart rate - cardiac arrest and fibrillation
- muscle spasm and contraction – e.g. inability to let go
- interference with ability to breathe
- electric burns – internal and external (entry and exit points)
- secondary effects – e.g. fall whilst working from ladder

Treatment of electric shock

The following are general guidelines on the treatment of electric shock

- raise the alarm
- switch off the power, if not possible, use insulating material to move victim from contact with the power supply
- place victim in recovery position
- call for an ambulance
- if trained give emergency first aid
- Cardio Pulmonary Resuscitation - CPR
- treat any burns
- remain with person until help arrives and constantly reassure person

The main causes of electrical fires in the workplace

- bad design, incorrect installation or wrong specification of fixed electrical installation
- lack of maintenance, testing, inspection, pat testing of electrical equipment
- sparking of switches, electric motors
- static electricity and lightening
- poor / damaged insulation
- incorrect fuse or circuit breaker
- damaged wiring
- loose connections
- using unauthorised equipment
- poor or no earth connection
- arching of breakers or switch gear
- overloading of system
- coiled cables / extension leads
- misuse of electrical equipment

Section 2: Control measures

In this section:

1. Control measures
2. Electrical Safety devices
3. Portable electrical equipment
4. Overhead power cables
5. Buried services

Learning Outcomes

Outline the control measures that should be taken when working with electrical systems or using electrical equipment in normal workplace conditions

General Controls - electricity

The following are the general controls for the use of electricity:

- design, construction and maintenance of electrical systems, work activities and protective equipment
- strength and capability of electrical equipment
- protection of equipment against adverse and hazardous environments
- insulation, protection and placing of electrical conductors
- earthing of conductors and other suitable precautions
- integrity of referenced conductors
- suitability of joints and connections used in electrical systems
- means for protection from excess current
- means for cutting off the supply and for isolation
- precautions to be taken for work on equipment made dead
- working on or near live conductors
- location of underground electrical services or 'hidden' services e.g. in walls
- adequate working space, access and lighting
- competence requirements for persons working on electrical equipment

Electrical safety devices

Earthing

- an 'earth' is an electrical connection to the ground (earth), often consisting of a wire attached to a metal rod inserted into the ground. Metal surfaces surrounding electrical equipment are often 'earthed'
- if a live wire 'touches' the metal part, the electricity should 'go to earth', therefore, 'blowing' or burning out the fuse, thereby cutting the electrical supply
- earth protects the equipment NOT the person

Residual current device

- Residual Current Device (RCD) is used to protect a person from an electric shock
- if there is a sudden change in current flow, the RCD cuts off within 40 milli seconds the electrical supply. The person will not therefore receive a fatal electric shock
- easy to test and rest
- difficult to defeat
- higher cost than a fuse

Fuse

- **fuse** – protects the equipment. Fitted in the live wire; if excessive current flows the fuse will 'blow', or burn out, therefore, breaking the circuit, hence the flow of electricity. But if a person touches a live part, they could receive an electric shock before the fuse blows
- cheap and simple to install

Double insulation

- **double insulation** – equipment designed in such a way that it does not require a safety connection to electrical

earth (ground). Usually achieved by having two layers of insulating material surrounding live parts or by using reinforced insulation
- **symbol** – one square inside another

Safe use of portable electrical equipment

Basic principles of Safe Use of 230-240V Portable Electrical Equipment i.e. equipment that has a plug:

- visual inspection before work. Check for faulty cables, extension leads (unwound), plugs, inadequate joints (e.g. taped), damage to external case, test label in date and sockets
- equipment not showing signs of faults / damage e.g. casing
- regular maintenance
- PAT (Portable Appliance Testing)
- don't use in flammable or damp atmospheres, e.g. in areas where highly flammable solvents are being used
- equipment only used for purpose it was designed for – do not misuse
- all equipment should be CE Marked
- modification / alterations to be done by competent person

Overhead power cables

Wherever possible avoid the need to work under or around overhead power lines. Where work cannot be avoided then the following considerations should be observed:

- if working on power cables, isolate the overhead power supply
- minimum of 6 meters away to prevent vehicle approach
- use permits to work - if appropriate

- erect goal posts to prevent arching of the electricity
- ensure that all danger zones are clearly marked with information signs and buntings
- use banksman, marshals or some other form of effective supervision
- prevent workers from using ladders or scaffolds
- physical restraints on mobile equipment to prevent boom pendant from swinging
- ensure that other vehicles booms are not in the prescribed distance limitations
- proximity warning devices are fitted and maintained in good working order
- supervision for all vehicles on site carrying out lifting operations
- barriers are conspicuous through marked barrels and bunting
- do not store any materials or equipment beneath the power lines

Buried services

The identification and location of all buried services must be carried out before any work commences. This information can be obtained through the health and safety file, historical drawings or design and installation records. The use of a Cable Avoidance Tool (CAT) scanner will ensure that the services, depth, and location have been identified.

Surface indicators as to the nature and location of the services can be indicated through physical markings e.g. paint spray marked areas, cones, stakes or buntings.

Safe digging practices (e.g. hand digging) observed at all times where high risk areas have been identified.

Chapter 11 - Fire safety

Section 1: Fire - basic principles, hazards and risks

In this section:

1. Responsible person
2. The Regulatory Reform (Fire Safety) Order 2005
3. The Fire triangle
4. Classification of fires
5. Principles of heat transfer
6. Common causes of fires

Learning outcomes

To know the main requirements of The Regulatory Reform (Fire Safety) Order 2005

Responsible person

The responsible person has control of the premises with duties often assigned to a manager, but responsibly lies with the controller.

Regulatory Reform (Fire Safety) Order 2005

The Order places duties on the Responsible Person, the main duties being:

- duty to take general fire precautions
- undertake risk assessment and apply the principles of prevention
- implement fire safety arrangements
- elimination or reduction of risks from dangerous substances, and additional emergency measures in respect of dangerous substances

- provision of fire-fighting and fire detection systems
- provision of emergency routes and exits
- provision of procedures for serious and imminent danger and for danger areas
- maintenance of equipment and systems
- provide appropriate safety assistance
- provision of information to employees and the self-employed
- provision of information and training
- co-operation and co-ordination

The Fire Triangle

A fire will only start if there are three elements:

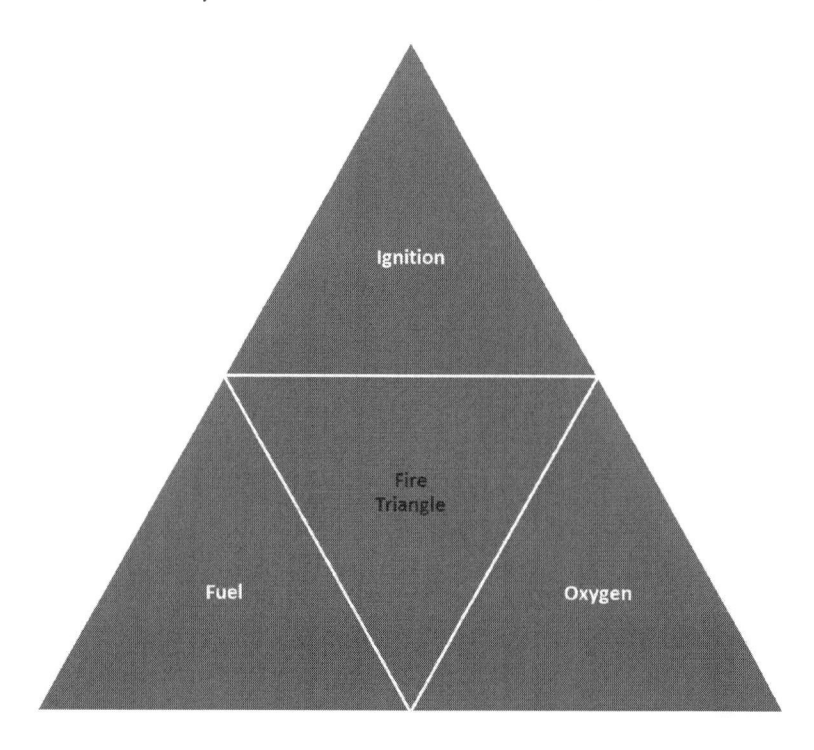

If a fire has started, remove one of the elements and the fire will extinguish by either:

- cooling it to reduce temperature
- starving it of fuel
- smothering it to exclude oxygen

Classification of fires

European	Fuel/Heat Source
Class A	Ordinary combustibles e.g. paper, wood
Class B	Flammable liquids e.g. petrol
Class C	Flammable gases e.g. acetylene
-	Electrical equipment
Class D	Combustible metals e.g. aluminium
Class F	Oil, cooking oil or fat

Principles of heat transfer

Fire (heat) is transferred in 4 separate ways:

- **Conduction** - spread of heat energy through solids
- **Convection** - heat transfer through a fluid or gas, involving expansion and movement
- **Radiation** - emission of heat energy through electromagnetic radiation in the infra-red part of the spectrum, which is then absorbed by matter
- **Direct Burning** - transfer of heat by direct contact with a burning or hot object

Common causes of fires

The common causes of fires in the workplace are:

- arson
- discarded cigarettes and matches
- faulty plant and equipment
- incorrect flammable liquids and materials storage and use
- hot processes e.g. hot works (welding)
- heating appliances e.g. cooking appliance left unattended
- combustible wastes not stored correctly or incompatibles put together

See also common causes of electrical fires

Section 2: Fire risk assessment

In this section:

1. Fire risk assessment process

Learning Outcomes

Outline the principles of fire risk assessment

Fire risk assessment - process

A 'responsible person' must carry out, and keep up to date, a fire risk assessment and implement appropriate measures to minimise the risk to life and property from fire.

The five steps in carrying out a fire risk assessment are the same for any risk process - **NOTE** detailed within the risk assessment section.

Step 1 - Identify hazards

How can a fire start? Consider the following

- sources of ignition e.g. smokers' material, matches and lighters; naked flames, arson
- flammable materials e.g. paper, flammable liquids
- sources of oxygen e.g. welding equipment, oxidising chemicals

Step 2 - Consider the people at risk

- employees, contractors, visitors and anyone who is vulnerable, e.g. disabled; young people
- consider also numbers of people affected

Step 3 - Assess risks and determine controls

- consider the hazards and people identified in previous two steps
- take action to remove and reduce risk to protect people and premises
- reduce the risk of fire starting e.g. machine maintenance, PAT testing, turn off machines not in use, storage of flammable materials
- reduce the risk of fire spreading e.g. protected escape routes, fire resistant doors and walls
- develop emergency procedures - appoint fire warden
- means of raising the alarm and contact emergency services
- fire-fighting equipment and location e.g. siting of extinguishers
- plan for an emergency e.g. signage, fire doors, assembly points, emergency lighting, etc.
- communication with neighbours e.g. if site of multiple occupancy

Step 4 - Record and provide training

- keep a record of the risks and action taken. This will be in the form of a fire plan for fire safety
- ensure that people understand what they need to do in the event of a fire
- inform, instruct and train people – all groups mentioned above
- conduct regular fire drills

Step 5 - Review

- regularly review your assessment
- check it takes into account of any changes on site

Section 3: Fire alarm and fire-fighting equipment

In this section:

1. Fire detection and warning
2. Fire-fighting equipment

Learning Outcomes

Identify the appropriate fire alarm system and fire-fighting equipment for a simple workplace

Fire detection and warning

Within any workplace an alarm system must be set up. Depending on the size and complexity of the site this may be:

- temporary or permanent mains operated fire alarm
- klaxon

- bell
- whistle
- shouting!

The warning needs to be distinctive, audible above other noise and recognisable by everyone

The means of raising the alarm must also be clearly communicated to employees, visitors, contractors etc.

Fire-fighting equipment

Factors to consider when siting fire-fighting equipment

- within 30m of any point in the building
- on escape routes and near exit doors
- at convenient height or on fibre-glass plinths
- clearly visible
- free from obstructions
- indicated by signs

Water
Red Body
- suitable for use on Class A Fires, wood, paper etc.
- not suitable for combustible liquids, cooking fats etc.
- not safe to use on fires involving electricity
- extinguishes by cooling

Foam
Cream body (Old type) or Red Body with Cream label (Newer Type)
- suitable for Class A and B Fires
- not suitable for use on fires involving electricity

- extinguishes by cooling and sealing the surface of a burning liquid

Powder

Blue body (Old type) or Red body with blue label (Newer Type)
- best on Class B fires but safe to use on any type of fire.
- works by chemically interfering with the combustion reaction by starving of oxygen

Carbon dioxide CO_2

Black body (Old type) or red body with black label (Newer type)
- best on Class B and C fires but safe to use on any type of fire
- safe to use on fires involving electricity
- extinguishes by reducing oxygen levels and cooling

Other types of extinguisher
- hose reels (water)
- fire blankets - e.g. used in kitchens for oil fires
- automatic sprinklers - fine water spray e.g. shops
- halon systems e.g. used in large computer rooms
- sand - suppressing metal fires e.g. from welding

Section 4: Evacuation of the workplace

In this section:

1. Emergency procedures
2. Roles of fire wardens
3. Provision of information
4. Building requirements

Learning Outcomes

Outline the factors which should be considered when implementing a successful evacuation of a workplace in the event of a fire

Emergency procedures

Responsible person must:

- establish appropriate procedures - formal policy, notices etc.
- arrange and record for safety drills
- nominate a sufficient number of competent persons (usually fire / emergency wardens) to implement procedures
- ensure appropriate information, instruction and training for all on site
- all persons on site are informed of the nature of the hazard (fire or emergency) and
- of the steps taken or
- to be taken to protect them from it
- regularly review procedures

Fire drills

The responsible person must produce emergency procedures and check they are working. This will include drills to test their efficacy which must be recorded and the results 'fed back' to the responsible person.

Roles of fire wardens

The Responsible Person must identify competent persons to assist them. These are usually called 'fire wardens', but can be emergency wardens, evacuation wardens or similar.
The primary duty of a Fire Warden is to ensure evacuation of 'their' part of the building and should be trained to:

- not put themselves at risk in carrying out their duties
- check all areas such as rooms, toilets and store rooms within their designated area
- encourage people to leave the building by the nearest available exit and direct people to the appropriate assembly point
- not use physical force or become involved in confrontation
- inform the responsible person (or representative) the area has been evacuated or somebody is remaining
- report any problems associated with the evacuation process to the responsible person
- report to the responsible person if disabled person is in the safe refuge

Provision of information

Employees, contractors, visitors etc. must know:

- the evacuation path for their work area
- alternative paths in the event an exit is blocked

- receive information on how to report a fire and whom to contact in an emergency
- location of fire-fighting equipment

Information can be provided by a variety of methods e.g.

- by the use of posters, notices, leaflets etc.
- by the use of signs, signals announcements etc.
- during induction programme

Building requirements

Key aspects to providing safe means of escape include:

Routes

- must be kept available and unobstructed
- wide enough to accommodate all people
- flow in one-direction
- doors that open outwards, easily opened and not locked
- routes must be well lit – consider emergency lighting
- well-separated, alternative ways to ground level and assembly point
- provide adequate signage e.g. above doors or at floor level depending on the environment

Protection

- routes can be protected by installing permanent fire separation, fire doors and non-flammable materials /walls
- provide 'safe refuges' for disabled people

Assembly

- escape routes give access to a safe place where people can assemble and be accounted for
- signs to indicate assembly point
- lighting should be provided for enclosed escape routes and emergency lighting may be required

Section 5: Highly flammable liquids

In this section:

1. Safe storage
2. Safe use

Learning Outcomes

Outline the factors which should be considered when storing and using flammable liquids

Safe storage

When storing in the workplace the following should be considered:

- remove sources of ignition e.g. no smoking
- suitable containers - metal containers with screw tops
- warning signs and labelling - containers and store
- easy access to spill kits
- emergency procedures developed
- keep away from processes and protect from sunlight
- flameproof storage area and use intrinsically safe electrical equipment
- bunded store, well ventilated, sump tray
- fire extinguishers close by

- segregate waste and empty containers
- secure area, restrict access
- PPE - flame retardant
- minimal amounts
- must not store more than 50 litres in a room

Safe use

When using the following should be considered:

- suitable containers - metal containers with screw tops
- warning signs and labelling - containers and store
- easy access to spill kits
- protect from sunlight and heat sources
- don't use close to hot processes or sources of ignition
- use in well ventilated
- fire extinguishers close by (e.g. powder or foam) and provide training in use of extinguisher
- segregate waste and empty containers
- restrict access
- minimal amounts
- store contaminated rags and papers in separate sealed metal container; NOT in general waste
- ensure competence of staff - especially in the risks of using

Chapter 12 - Chemical and Biological Health Hazards and Control

Section 1: Forms and classification of hazardous substances

In this section:

1. Chemical and biological agents
2. Sources of information

Learning Outcomes

Outline the forms of, the classification of, and health risks from exposure to hazardous substances

Chemical forms

Chemicals are found in the following forms:

- dusts - respirable 0.5μm to 0.7μm e.g. wood dust
- fumes - <1μm e.g. welding fume (Very small particles)
- gases
- mists - Liquid droplets >20μm
- vapour
- liquids

Biological forms

Biological Agents can exist as any one of the following forms:

Fungi

Example	Health Effect	Source
Aspergillus spores	Can cause complications for people with weakened immune systems	Present in air

Bacteria

Example	Health Effect	Source
Legionellosis - the collective name given to the pneumonia-like illness caused by legionella	Sever flu-like symptoms	Cooling towers; evaporating condensers; spa pools; hot water systems used in all sorts of premises (work and domestic) especially where there are 'dead ends' or standing / stagnant water; showers heads

Viruses

Example	Health Effect	Source
Hepatitis B and HIV	sever flu like symptoms	exposed to contaminated needles, body fluids e.g. care workers, doctors, nurses, persons picking up litter

Prions

A prion is an infectious agent composed of protein in a misfolded form.

Example	Health Effect	Source
Transmissible - spongiform encephalopathies in a variety of mammals, including bovine spongiform encephalopathy (BSE - "mad cow disease"). In humans, prions cause Creutzfeldt-Jakob Disease (CJD)	Triggers a chain reaction that produces large amounts of the prion. In infected tissue, causing tissue damage and cell death	Consuming infected meat

Controls of biological forms

- cleaning and disinfection
- personal hygiene - washing hands, no hand-to-mouth movements
- PPE - e.g. respirator, overalls
- Immunisation
- vermin control
- immunisation
- health surveillance
- engineering controls - e.g. LEV, glove box, enclosure
- water treatment
- effective waste disposal
- no eating, drinking or smoking
- CJD (prions) - screening of meat sources

Sources of information

The following are the primary sources of information about hazardous substances:

Container labels

Should contain the following:

- substance identification; name of substance, chemical name and any 'common' name.
- precautions
- risk phrase
- hazard symbol
- company manufacturing / supplying details

Material safety data sheets

Produced by manufacturers and should contain the following information:

- substance identification – name of substance, chemical name and any 'common' name.
- company manufacturing / supplying details
- risk phrase e.g. R32 - contact with acids liberates very toxic gas
- hazards identification
- composition / information on ingredients
- first-aid measures
- fire-fighting measures
- accidental release measures
- handling and storage
- exposure controls / personal protection
- physical and chemical properties
- stability and reactivity
- storage precautions
- toxicological information
- ecological information
- disposal considerations
- transport information regulatory information
- other information

Risk phrases

On the labels of bottles and Material Safety Data Sheets (MSDS), each chemical is assigned a Risk Phrase and corresponding code e.g.

- R32 Contact with acids liberates very toxic gas
- R33 Danger of cumulative effects
- R34 Causes burns

Classification of hazardous substances

Symbol	Abbreviation	Hazard	Description of Hazard
	E	Explosive	Chemicals that explode
	O	Oxidising	Chemicals that react exothermically with other chemicals
	F +	extremely flammable	Chemicals that have an extremely low flash point and boiling point, and gases that catch fire in contact with air
	F	highly flammable	Chemicals that may catch fire with air, only need brief contact with an ignition source, have a very low flash point or evolve highly flammable gases in contact with water
	T +	very toxic	Chemicals that at very low levels cause damage to health
	T	toxic	Chemicals that at low levels cause damage to health
	Xn	harmful	Chemicals that may cause damage to health
	C	corrosive	Chemicals that may destroy living tissue on contact
	Xi	irritant	Chemicals that may cause inflammation to the skin or other mucous membranes

Section 2: Assessment of health risks

In this section:

1. Routes of entry into the body
2. Factors to be considered

Learning Outcomes

Explain the factors to be considered when undertaking an assessment of the health risks from substances commonly encountered in the workplace

Routes of entry into the body

Means of entry into body

- **Inhalation** – breathed in and entry the blood stream via the alveoli of the lungs. Can also affect the lungs and plural cavity. E.g. petrol vapours, asbestos fibres.
- **Ingestion** – ingested into the body and blood system via the stomach.
- **Absorption** – can pass directly through (without breaking or corroding) the skin into the blood stream. E.g. mineral oil; which can give risk to testicular cancer.
- **Direct entry** – through wounds and direct injection
- **Direct skin contact** – can affect the skin e.g. cement giving rise to dermatitis

Chronic and acute effects

Acute health effects are characterized by sudden and severe exposure and rapid absorption of the substance. Normally, a single large exposure is involved. Acute health effects are often reversible. Examples: carbon monoxide or cyanide poisoning.

Chronic health effects are characterized by prolonged or repeated exposures over many days, months or years. Symptoms may not be immediately apparent. Chronic health effects are often irreversible. Examples: lead or mercury poisoning.

Cellular defense mechanism

The first line of defense from attack by hazardous substances and biological agents are:

- **skin** is an excellent line of defense because it provides an almost impenetrable biological barrier protecting the internal environment.
- **clotting of blood** near open wounds prevents an open space for antigens to easily enter the organism by coagulating the blood.
- **mucus and cilia** found in the nose and throat can catch foreign agents entering these open cavities then sweep them outside via coughing, sneezing and vomiting.

If these first lines of defense fail, then there are further defenses found within the body to ensure that the foreign agent is eliminated e.g.

- **white blood cells** provide a means of attacking foreign material by 'engulfing them'.

Control measures

- disinfecting and cleaning
- vermin control
- personal hygiene, washing of hands, cover cuts and wounds
- no eating, no drinking, no smoking
- use of appropriate PPE e.g. respirator
- immunisation
- health surveillance
- engineering controls e.g. LEV, containments, glove boxes
- site monitoring, procedures
- appropriate information, instruction and training, supervision

Assessments - factors to consider

- chemical or biological hazard
- form of the hazardous substance - solid, liquid, gas, dust etc.
- hazardous nature of the substance, toxic, harmful etc. and EH 40 contains toxicological data
- concentration and duration of exposure
- health effects - severity and likelihood
- mode of entry into the body
- health of the person e.g. sensitisation
- number of people exposed and age, gender of the person (e.g. pregnant women must not work with lead) or existing conditions
- frequency and duration of exposure
- compatibility issues e.g. some chemicals when mixed react together
- location of use
- consideration of effectiveness or existing controls

Section 3: Workplace Exposure Limits (WELs)

In this section:

1. Purpose of WELs
2. Threshold limit values

Learning Outcomes

Describe the use and limitations of Workplace Exposure Limits including the purpose of long term and short term exposure limits

Purpose of Work Exposure Limits (WELs)

Designed to control the exposure to a variety of potentially dangerous substances.

EH 40

EH40/2005 Workplace exposure limits, published by the HSE, sets the WELs for hazardous substances.

Threshold limit values

- limits that a person can be exposed to each working day that will not have a detrimental effect to health either in the short term or long term
- measured in concentrations of parts per million (ppm) e.g. Time Weighted Average (TWA); can be a short term period of 15 minutes or a long term period of 8 hours
- long term 8 hour average is used to protect workers from the chronic ill health effects of the substance
- short term limits are used to protect against the acute effects of contact with a substance causing ill health, such as eye irritation, which may occur in minutes or even seconds of exposure

Section 4: Control measures

In this section:

1. Principles of good practice
2. LEV systems

Learning Outcomes

Outline control measures that should be used to reduce the risk of ill-health from exposure to hazardous substances

Duty to reduce exposure

UK Law requires employers to prevent exposure, or where this is not possible to reduce the risks of exposure as far as is reasonably practicable or to adequately control the risks to health. Examples of risk control include:

- avoid or eliminate the substance, reduce exposure time, isolate the substance, engineering controls established
- any process to be designed to minimise the emissions, their release, or spread of a substance
- take into consideration the routes of entry
- provide appropriate controls for the health risks
- appropriate Personal Protective Equipment readily available
- monitoring control systems and their effectiveness
- information and training for all exposed workers
- additional controls are not creating further risks to health or safety

Principles of good practice

The following summarises good practice for implementing control measures

- elimination or substitution of hazardous substances or form of substance
- process changes
- reduced time exposure; significance of time weighted averages
- enclosure of hazards; segregation of process and people
- Local Exhaust Ventilation (LEV): general applications and principles of capture and removal of hazardous substances; components of a basic system and factors that may reduce its effectiveness; requirements for inspection

- use and limitations of dilution ventilation
- respiratory protective equipment: purpose, application and effectiveness; types of equipment and their suitability for different substances; selection, use and maintenance
- other protective equipment and clothing (gloves, overalls, eye protection)
- personal hygiene and protection regimes
- health surveillance and biological monitoring

LEV systems

A Local Exhaust Ventilation system (LEV) takes dusts, mists, gases, vapour or fumes out of the air so that they are removed from the atmosphere and hence cannot be breathed in, or contaminate areas where they could cause harm or come in contact with people. An LEV system should:

- collect the air that contains the contaminants:
- make sure they are contained and taken away from people
- clean the air (if necessary) and get rid of the contaminants safely
- testing - every 14 months with written records

Section 5: Specific agents

In this section:

3. Asbestos
4. Blood born viruses
5. Carbon monoxide
6. Cement
7. Legionella
8. Leptospirosis
9. Silica
10. Hard and soft wood dusts

Learning Outcomes

Outline the hazards, risks and controls associated with specific agents

Asbestos

Health effects

Health effects are due to the fibres (like spears) penetrating

- trachea or wind pipe - cancer
- lungs - asbestosis
- chest lining – mesothelioma
- abdomen - mesothelioma

Where is asbestos found?

- asphalt roofing
- acoustic ceiling tiles
- window putty
- textured paint or plaster
- interior or exterior walls
- electrical switch gear
- lagging of pipes or around heaters
- under floor materials
- floor tiles
- gaskets in heaters

Exposure

Normally due to:

- material being disturbed or the material becomes fibrous and 'breaks-down' which is often called 'friable'

- otherwise - no fibres are created, therefore 'best sealed' by e.g. painting and left alone until suitable time to remove.

Controls

All asbestos containing materials that are located / found must:

- be recorded - Asbestos Register
- be identified by the use of markings or labels
- provide a Permit to Work and a written safe system of work and a plan provided for all workers involved
- training provided to those that may be at risk including maintenance engineers, or installation engineers
- all workers to be briefed upon hazards with the specific asbestos

Asbestos register

All employers have the duty to manage asbestos by the following measures:

- carry out a survey to determine there are materials containing asbestos in non-domestic premises, if so, the amounts, location and condition
- to presume that materials contain asbestos till proved otherwise
- record the location, and condition of the asbestos that has been presumed to be asbestos containing materials
- assess risks to any person being exposed to fibres from those materials
- prepare a detailed plan of how the materials contain asbestos will be managed
- take necessary measures to implement the action plan
- at suitable intervals monitor and review the action plan for effectiveness

- provide information regarding any asbestos containing materials to any person who is likely to disturb the materials e.g. plumbers

Blood born viruses

Specific Agents / where found	Symptoms / Health Effect	Occupations at Risk	Precautions
• mainly found in bloods or bodily fluids • includes HIV Aids, • Hepatitis B & C	• HIV causes the immune system to fail	• worker that comes into contact with human bodily fluids e.g. doctors, nurses	• good personal hygiene • avoid sharps • effective PPE • waste disposal techniques • training for all persons potentially affected • monitoring worker exposure • reporting procedures • immunisation where possible • use of long-sleeve shirts or overalls

Carbon monoxide (CO)

where found/details	Symptoms / Health Effect	Occupations at Risk	Precautions
• colorless, odorless and tasteless gas • produced by the incomplete combustion of carbons e.g. room with gas fire badly ventilated	• flu like symptoms, nausea, severe headaches • unconsciousness • could be fatal • person goes red in the face	• central heating engineer • garage workers - with engine running	• CO monitors • training / competence of workers • ventilation • servicing of equipment

223

Cement

Details	Symptoms / Health Effect	Occupations at Risk	Precautions
• widely used in the construction industry • part of the mortar and concrete mix	• corrosive (alkaline) • contact with the skin causes contact dermatitis and serious chemical burns • inflammation of the respiratory tract • damage to the mucus membrane	• construction and demolition workers, bricklayers, concrete laying	• PPE e.g. gloves • Good hygiene, welfare facilities • training monitoring and supervision

Legionella

where found	Symptoms / Health Effect	Occupations at Risk	Precautions
• bacterium • frequently found in water e.g. cooling towers, domestic hot water (dead ends), air conditioning units, stagnant water systems, shower heads in hotels • multiply in slurry or sludge, scale, algae, rust and a temperature of 20 – 50 degrees C	• aching muscles, headaches and fever, including severe coughing, confusion and delirium	• bathing in contaminated water • maintenance workers • hotel and hospital workers	• good hygiene • welfare facilities • training monitoring and supervision • use of biocides, chemical treatment in systems • heating water above 60 degrees C

Leptospirosis

Specific Agents / where found	Symptoms / Health Effect	Occupations at Risk	Precautions
• **Leptospirosis bacterium** • **Weil's disease** - transmitted to humans by contact with urine from infected rats • **Hardjo** form of leptospirosis is transmitted from cattle to humans • **Cattle worker's leptospirosis**	• both diseases start with a flu-like illness with a persistent and severe headache • leads to vomiting and muscle pains • ultimately to jaundice, meningitis and kidney failure	• workers exposed to rats, rat or cattle urine • working near stagnant water infested by rats • farmers, vets, meat inspectors butchers, abattoir, sewer works, sewers, ditches • training and information • carry and distribute advice cards	• get rid of rats • don't touch rats with unprotected hands • cover cuts and broken skin with water proof plaster • if contact, wash cuts / grazes • PPE e.g. gloves • personal hygiene • wash hands before eating, drinking, smoking • early reporting to doctor

Silica

where found	Symptoms / Health Effect	Occupations at Risk	Precautions
• cutting, grinding, drilling, blasting of natural or manmade minerals containing Silica's e.g. paving stones	• Silicosis – cancer of lungs	• mining and quarrying operations • construction worker cutting paving stones with Disc Cutter	• dust suppression • PPE e.g. respiratory breathing apparatus • welfare facilities • health promotion and health surveillance • use of LEV system

Hard and soft wood dusts

Specific Agents / where found	Symptoms / Health Effect	Occupations at Risk	Precautions
• Hard and Soft wood dusts Wood cutters, forestry, furniture manufacturers	• Hardwood dust can cause cancer, particularly of the nose • Hard wood dust can cause serious health problems including respiratory health problems such as asthma, dermatitis and allergic reactions • Soft wood dust is mainly a nuisance but affects people with inherent breathing difficulties	• Carpenters and joiners are more likely to be affected, also wood mills and forestry workers	• Ensure that hardwood dusts do not exceed the Workplace Exposure Limit (WEL) of 5mg/m3 • Local exhaust ventilation, vacuuming • Respiratory protection equipment • Supervision and monitoring health

Section 6: Safe handling and storage of waste

In this section:

1. Basic principles of storage

Learning Outcomes

Outline the basic requirements related to the safe handling and storage of waste.

Principles of storage

Controlled waste

- is described as any waste arising from domestic, industrial or commercial premises.

Hazardous waste

- is described as any waste that may be harmful to human health and / or the environment. In order to ensure that wastes are adequately stored and transported the following considerations should be applied by all businesses.
- all wastes are stored and transported appropriately and securely so that it does not allow any wastes to escape
- any person or business handling such wastes are authorised to do so
- waste transfer notes are to be completed and records kept for 2 years
- ensure that the wastes have been taken to a waste collection point that is authorised to accept it

Site storage

- provision of a safe system of work to deal with different types of hazardous waste is developed
- records and inventories of locations where hazardous wastes are stored
- ensuring that waste streams are identified and separated by type
- incompatible wastes are not mixed or stored in the same vicinity
- hazardous and non-hazardous wastes are to be kept separate and should not be mixed
- all wastes should be kept in a space provided for that purpose that is spacious, secure and protected from the elements of weather
- all wastes are to be stored is suitable containers
- drip trays or bunded areas are established to ensure the containment of a liquid waste

- adequate and appropriate warning signs and clearly marked labels identifying the nature of the waste
- person working with waste should be provided with appropriate information, instructions and training
- provision of suitable types or forms of personal protective equipment and spares kept
- spill procedures
- emergency procedures

Waste transfer

- wastes should only be transported by a registered waste carrier
- only be transported to a facility that holds suitable environmental permits
- wastes accompanied by a transfer note
- consignment note has been completed for hazardous wastes
- records (and copies) are kept for auditing purposes

Chapter 13 - Physical and Psychological Health Hazards and Risk Control

Section 1: Noise

In this section:

1. Noise - basic principles
2. Noise levels
3. Control of noise

Learning Outcomes

Outline the health effects associated with exposure to noise and appropriate control measures

Noise - basic principles

What is noise?

Noise is regarded as any sound that is loud, unpleasant or undesired.

The following are common occupations with potential for excessive noise exposure:

- construction – e.g. use of machinery such as pneumatic impact tools
- uniformed services e.g. use of small arms
- entertainment – e.g. in discos
- manufacturing e.g. when using production machinery
- call centres e.g. continual use of head phones

Physical and psychological effects

Acute Effects (Short term / reversible / effects quickly noticed)	Chronic Effects (Long term / non-reversible / effect not noticed immediately)
Tinnitus – (ringing in the ears)	Tinnitus – (ringing in the ears)
Noise Induced Hearing Loss – resulting in Temporary Threshold Shift (inability to hear certain frequencies) which can lead to mis-hearing words, and not being able to hear conversations in a crowded room	Noise Induced Hearing Loss – resulting in Temporary Threshold Shift (inability to hear certain frequencies) which can lead to mis-hearing words, and not being able to hear conversations in a crowded room
Secondary effects – being distracted and then being injured e.g. falling off a ladder	Damage to the hairs in the cochlea (inner ear)
Physical damage to ear drum e.g. rupture	Occupations Deafness – significant hearing loss – over 50dB

Measurement of noise

Noise is measured in decibels (dB).

- **'A-weighting'** written as dB(A), is used to measure average noise levels
- **'C-weighting'** or dB(C), to measure peak, impact or explosive noises
- the scales are not LINEAR but LOGARITHMIC, therefore, for every THREE decibel increase in level the sound level DOUBLES

dB(A)	dB(C)
• Mimicking the human ear • Filters out low frequencies • Slightly emphasizes upper middle frequencies around 2-3 kHz	• Almost un-weighted • Slight filtering at high and low frequencies • High sound pressure levels - aircraft noise

Typical noise levels

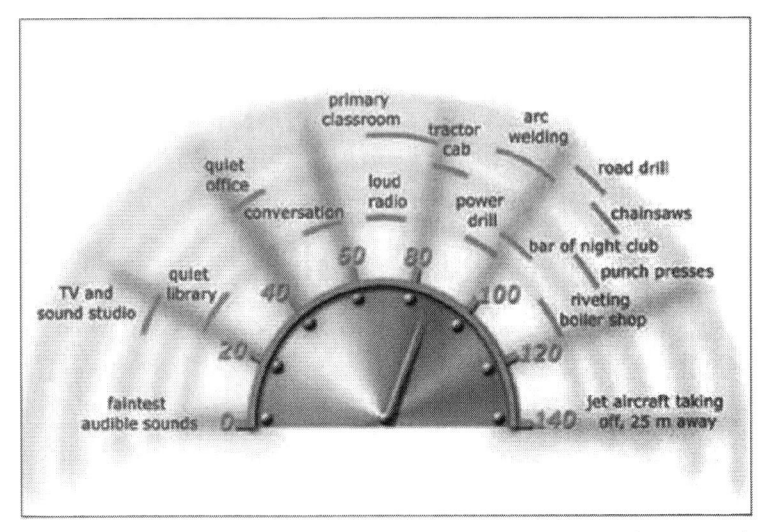

Source – UK HSE

Control of noise

Noise can be controlled by one of three methods by reducing sound levels:

- At **Source** – e.g. regular maintenance of equipment
- During **Path** taken by the sound – e.g. use of acoustic tiles
- At the **Individual** – e.g. use of Personal Protective Equipment

Typical noise abatement

- eliminate the noise by changing the process
- using quieter equipment or a different, quieter process
- engineering/technical controls to reduce, at source, the noise produced by a machine or process

- using screens, barriers, enclosures and absorbent materials to reduce the noise on its path to the people exposed
- designing and laying out the workplace to create quiet workstations
- improved working techniques to reduce noise levels
- limiting the time people spend in noisy areas

PPE

When selecting PPE for attenuating noise the following must be considered:

- suitability for the work
- compatibility with other safety equipment
- pattern of the noise exposure
- need to communicate / hear warning sounds
- environmental factors
- cost of maintenance or replacement
- comfort and user preference
- medical condition of the wearer

NOTE - PPE does not eliminate the noise, it only reduces (called attenuation) specific frequency level.
Therefore, consideration must be given to the noise reduction required and the frequency of the noise to be attenuated

Health surveillance

Audiometric testing is required to monitor a person's hearing to determine if these is any long-term damage taking place

- often takes place at recruitment and at pre-determined intervals

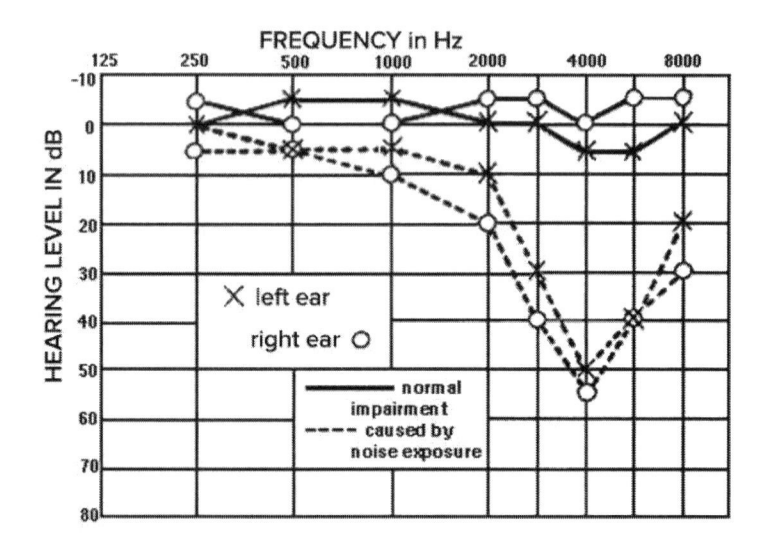

Section 2: Vibration

In this section:

1. Whole body vibration
2. Hand Arm Vibration (HAV)
3. Control of vibration

Learning Outcomes

Outline the health effects associated with exposure to vibration and appropriate control measures

Whole body vibration

Whole body vibration is the shaking or jolting of the human body through a supporting surface (usually a seat or the floor) driving or riding on a vehicle along an unmade road

Acute effects - short term

- back pain - conditions made worst
- abdominal pain or general feeling of discomfort, including headaches, chest pain, nausea and loss of balance
- insomnia
- shaking after exposure

Chronic effects - long term

- disc displacement, degenerative spinal changes, lumbar scoliosis, degenerative disorders of the spine and disorders of the gastrointestinal system

Controls

- reduce use of high vibration or jolting equipment or machines
- maintenance of equipment
- purchase equipment with lower vibration
- reduce exposure time e.g. job rotation
- reduce grip on tool
- gloves to keep hands warm
- health surveillance
- training so users can recognise possible effects and controls

Hand Arm Vibration

Hand Arm Vibration (HAV) transmitted from work processes into workers' hands and arms often associated with operating handheld power tools

Effects

- affects nerves, blood vessels, muscles and joints of the hand, wrist and arm
- blanching / Vibration White Finger (VWF)
- severe pain in the affected fingers
- involuntary muscle movements
- reduced strength and grip
- Carpal Tunnel Syndrome
- pain, tingling, numbness and weakness in parts of the hand

Risk factors

- frequency of the vibration
- 2 to 1,500 Hz is potentially damaging
- 5 to 20 Hz is most dangerous
- strength of the grip and other forces
- duration of exposure
- frequency of exposure
- low temperature
- individual factors

Control of vibration

- purchase equipment with less vibration
- measurement of levels
- reduce time of exposure
- job rotation
- maintenance of equipment
- health surveillance
- damping of equipment
- use of PPE e.g. gloves to keep hands warm
- information, instruction and training
- supervision of staff

Section 3: Radiation

In this section:

1. Types and sources of radiation
2. Radon

Learning Outcomes

Outline the principal health effects associated with heat, ionising and non-ionising radiation and basic protection techniques

Types and sources of radiation

Radiation is either ionising or non-ionising:

Ionising

- shorter wavelength, higher frequency and more energy than non-ionising radiation
- can penetrate solid matter (but very dense solids e.g. Lead can absorb)
- affects atoms and can form ions (charged particles)

	IONISING		
	(Affects the cell structure by ionising the atoms i.e. removes the electrons)		
Name	**Common Occupational Sources**	**Occupational Risk**	**Control Measures**
• Alpha (α) • Beta (β) • Gamma (δ)	• Produced from x-ray sets • Radioactive substances • Typically used in medical exposures, industrial radiography equipment and gauges used in industrial process control • Also be produced from naturally occurring radioactive substances including radon gas.	• Dermatitis • Burns • Cell damage • Cataracts • Damage DNA and can cause health effects such as cancer, later in life	• Health Monitoring • Shielding e.g. lead screen • Distance from the source • Exposure time reduced • PPE – e.g. Lead Apron • Segregation • Competence of users • LEV • Enclosure e.g. glove box
• X-rays	• Ultrasonic, non-destructive testing		• Health Monitoring • Shielding e.g. lead screen • Distance from the source • Reduced Exposure time • Segregation • Competence of users

Non-Ionising

- has low penetrating power and does not affect atoms and form ions

The electromagnetic spectrum provides an overview of the types of energy waves. Radiation can also be:

- **waves** - e.g. gamma rays, x-rays
- **particles** - e.g. alpha particles or beta particles

NON-IONISING			
Name	Common Occupational Sources	Occupational Risk	Control Measures
• InfraRed (IR)	• Very hot, glowing sources in glass and metal production	• Skin burns • Cataracts	• Health Monitoring • Shielding • Distance from the source • Exposure time reduced • PPE – e.g. Goggles
• Ultra Violet (UV) rays	• Welding • The sun • Tanning studios	• Skin burns • Skin cancer • Conjunctivitis • Arc eye	• Health Monitoring • Shielding • Distance from the source • Exposure time reduced • PPE – e.g. Welding visor • Sun cream for outside workers
• Radiofrequency and microwaves	• Communications transmitters	• Heating of any exposed part of the body	• Health Monitoring • Shielding • Distance from the source • Exposure time reduced
• Visible radiation from high-intensity light sources	• LASERs	• Permanent, severe damage to the eye and skin	• Health Monitoring • Shielding • Exposure time reduced • Use low energy source

Radon

Naturally occurring radioactive gas and has no smell, taste or colour. Decay product of uranium and is naturally occurring and rises from the soil into the air. Outdoors radon is diluted and poses a low risk. When it builds up in enclosed spaces such as in cellars or spaces under floors of a building it can potentially cause a greater problem especially where there is ventilation.

Some of the workplaces that are at risk include:

- sumps; basements / cellars; pits; sewers; wells; underground tunnels and voids At risk groups include people working in
- water utility; mines; tunnels

Controls

Combination of:

- **measurement** – test for Radon
- **surveillance** – continue monitoring until remedial action is complete
- **risk assessment** – set priorities for action based on radon levels
- **mitigation** – e.g. forced ventilation, insulate basements
- **maintenance** – conduct periodic testing and routine checks

Section 4: Stress

In this section:

1. Cause and effect
2. Risk assessment and controls

Learning Outcomes

Outline the causes and effects of stress at work and appropriate control actions

Causes and effects of stress

Work related stress develops when a person finds it difficult to cope with the demands being placed on them.

All stress is not work related but can be 'imported' due to social or personal issues.

It can be a significant cause of illness and is known to be linked to high levels of sickness absence, staff turnover and a cause of accidents caused by Human Error.

Identifying and Controlling Stress is a process of Risk Assessment, the same as other risk assessments, after all - stress is a Hazard.

What can increase stress levels?

- unrealistic targets
- fear of redundancy
- lack of management support
- organisation change
- poor health and safety standards
- lack of welfare
- peer pressure / bullying
- personal issues
- lack of training
- poor supervision
- poor pay
- lack of incentives
- poor safety culture
- monotonous job

Risk assessment and control of stress

Step 1 - identify the hazards

- **Demands** placed upon the individual and includes, workload, work patters, and the work environment
- **Control** – how much say or control a person has in the way they do their work
- **Support** – how much support is the individual is given in terms of encouragement, sponsorship and resources provided to assist them doing the job, line management and colleagues (peers)

- **Role** - whether people understand their role within the organisation and whether the organisation ensures that they do not have conflicting roles
- **Change** – how organisational change is managed and communicated to people
- **Relationships** - promoting positive working to avoid conflict and dealing with unacceptable behaviour. That is promoting a positive Safety Culture

Step 2 - decide who can be harmed

- undertake surveys
- refer to sickness absence data; staff turnover rates; exit interviews and number of referrals to occupational health
- reference information from staff meetings, communications etc.

Step 3 - determine controls - considerations

- providing employees with adequate and achievable demands in relation to the agreed hours of work
- people's skills and abilities are matched to the job demands
- jobs are designed to be within the capabilities of employees
- addressing employees' concerns about their work environment are addressed
- giving specific groups of employees more control over aspects of their work
- improving communication up and down the management chain, and between groups
- management development, particularly in interpersonal skills
- job reviews/task analysis using the Management Standards as a framework

- updating a specific policy or procedure shown to have failings

Step 4 - record findings

- record the findings of the risk assessment

Step 5 - evaluate and review

- evaluate the whole process and review to determine if appropriate or improvements can be made

About the Author

Richard is a Chartered Health and Safety Practitioner with over 30 years' experience of the Health and Safety NEBOSH Qualification.

He has written this book as an essential health and safety reference based on the NEBOSH General Certificate.

Therefore, if you are studying towards the NEBOSH *'General Certificate in Occupational Safety and Health'*, study this and PASS! Or use it as a handy-reference.

Also appropriate for study towards other NEBOSH certificate courses when there is a common syllabus e.g. International Certificate, and other relevant Health and Safety qualifications.

For further information about Richard visit:
www.richardbutler.info

Printed in Great Britain
by Amazon